THE URBAN COYOTE

Howlings
on Family, Community
and the Search for Peace and Quiet

THE URBAN COYOTE

Howlings
on Family, Community
and the Search for Peace and Quiet

by JAMES P. LENFESTEY

NODIN PRESS

Cover art by Roger Boehm

ISBN: 0-931714-86-9

Library of Congress Card Number: 99-068388

First Edition

Nodin Press, a division of Micawber's Inc.
525 North Third Street
Minneapolis, MN 55401

To my family, community and the many dedicated volunteers of the Hill and Lake Press, a true neighborhood newspaper.

INTRODUCTION

What These Columns Are, and Aren't

The columns I wrote as the Urban Coyote over fifteen years tell the kinds of stories that don't get into mainstream newspapers, where I worked for seven years as an editorial writer, for they don't present news but context. No cataclysms are described in this collection, nor even events of unusual human interest. Instead this book catalogues the ordinary ripples of birth, graduation, marriage and death in the life of a family and community. Some columns uncover small triumphs of neighbors over curbs and raccoons over neighbors, explore the communal repercussions of baseball and the State Fair and offer a guide for creating a block party and reading group. Others share in the grief of neighbors losing children and chronicle attempts to cool the hectic pace of life by joining a church, writing poetry or lingering in the cold waters of a lake.

Together these very short true stories add up to one person's experience of living for twenty-five years in a particular urban neighborhood— one in which raising a family and cleaving together as a community are not nostalgic fantasies of a bygone era but a vital urban way of life.

I am pleased to have had the chance to tell such stories.

A note on the selection of columns:

The editors and I tried to pick columns that would resonate for readers outside as well as inside the community in which they were published — four neighborhoods near downtown Minneapolis in which the Hill and Lake Press distributes 6000 copies ten times a year. Most of the columns have been revised, some extensively. All but one appeared originally in the Hill and Lake Press. Several won awards from the Neighborhood and Community Press Association.

Special gratitude to Miriam Feldman, Sara Saetre and Thomas R. Smith for their editing help and encouragement.

James P. Lenfestey
The Urban Coyote

Acknowledgements:

"A Solstice Call" was first published in the StarTribune and is reprinted by permission of the StarTribune, Minneapolis St. Paul.

Poem number 39, by Han-shan, translated by Burton Watson, copyright 1962 Burton Watson, copyright 1970 Columbia University Press, used by permission.

"A Story That Could Be True," copyright 1993 by the estate of William Stafford, used by permission.

"You Who Never Arrived," from *Selected Poetry of Rainer Maria Rilke,* translated by Stephen Mitchell, Random House, copyright 1989. Used by permission.

Contents

Part Two
CENTER OF THE NEIGHBORHOOD
1988–89

Part Three
COYOTE COOLS OUT
1990–92

Part Four
A HIGH AND HOLY CALLING
1993–94

Part Five
DEJA VU ALL OVER AGAIN
1995–96

Part Six
THE END OF A GOOD SUMMER
1997–99

PART ONE

ΘZYMANDIAS
UNDER THE ELMS

1984–87

Ozymandias
Under the Elms

(May 1984)

I met a traveler from an antique land
Who said: Two vast and trunkless legs of stone
Stand in the desert . . .

Percy Bysshe Shelley's "Ozymandias" is the one of the few poems I successfully memorized in high school. The sonnet is a powerful mocking of human shortsightedness. I wonder why that poem came back to me today?

The most recent "traveler" to my neighborhood is my 76-year-old mother, making her first visit to inspect our new house. The "antique land" then, must be her hometown and mine, DePere, Wisconsin, a small town of 8,000 people nestled along the industrial Fox River four miles south of Green Bay.

She lives on North Broadway, a classic small town main street over which hundred-year-old elms once arched its entire length. The cool green precision of the canopy gave each house the aspect of an English country estate arrayed with sycamores, a French chateau lined with Lombardy poplars or an ante-bellum Southern mansion entered through a corridor of live oaks.

Soon after her arrival here, I took her out for a walk

around our Minneapolis neighborhood. As we strolled, I pointed out the varied architectural styles of houses built as early as the 1880's and as late as the 1950's, and told her stories of some of the neighbors we'd come to know. Suddenly she stopped and tugged on my arm. "Jim," she said, looking up in disbelief, "That's an elm tree!"

Indeed, elegant elm trees shaded the blocks all around us just as they do back home. Then I remembered. The magnificent elm trees of North Broadway are dead, every one. They were strangled to death by Dutch Elm Disease, the dreaded DED, a blight accidentally brought from Europe and sweeping across the country from the East.

Mother was delighted and bereft at once—delighted by the glory of our urban arbor, miserable at the loss she remembered from home. The stately avenue of North Broadway now looks like a fresh suburban street or a sun-baked Las Vegas strip. No trees. No shade. No shadows. No green. Now sadly accustomed to their absence, she did not expect to see elms anywhere in the Midwest.

My mother's reaction made me both frightened and proud. Around here we can still stroll in the shade of elms, I told her, and it's no accident. This neighborhood still has living elms because we are part of an enlightened local effort to keep them alive.

Our state, upon learning of the impending DED epidemic advancing through Wisconsin, set up the most sophisticated statewide shade tree pest-control program in the nation. The plan included funds to identify and remove infected elms as soon as possible, as the beetles that spread the fungus breed only in dead elm wood.

Unfortunately, this year the Minnesota legislature, under a budget-cutting imperative, declared that the funding for the elm removal program had to die. The same state government that put Minnesota in the forefront of treating many social and environmental diseases recanted on this one in spite of ferocious lobbying by neighbor Don Willeke among others. Willeke, a lawyer and tenacious advocate for the urban forest, argued that if we don't slow the elm blight now with a swift sanitation program, Minnesotans will have to remove the dead trees anyway later at greater cost. His irrefutable logic—borne out by DePere's sad experience—is that spending a little saves a lot over time. But budget cutting has a logic all its own.

Fortunately, we are part of an exceptionally enlightened urban neighborhood. Volunteers have set up block-based elm-watch and elm-sweep programs. An ad hoc neighborhood committee organizes a social event once a year, the "Beetle Bash," that raises funds to trim the neighborhood elms and organize volunteer disposal of infected wood.

Fortunately too, state scientists have developed a fungistat that appears to prevent the spread of the tree-killing fungus once a tree has been infected. Injected in spring near the roots, the fungus-stopping effects last for two or three years before a new injection is needed, long enough to maintain a lot of cooling shade. Most neighbors make the effort to use it.

Forces from the laboratory to the grass-roots have combined to save our graceful sheltering giants, at least for a while.

So when residents of the neighborhood visit sadly denuded communities in the Midwest, or suburbs with sprigs for trees, or baking desert towns, we can honorably express shock at the tragic lack of cooling vegetation. An occasional "Darn, it's hot in the sun here," or "Gosh, that unobstructed wind has a nasty bite to it," can be forgiven, but only as long as one's own trees are still around to be smug about and snug under. Only if our urban neighborhood continues to maintain our physical place and sense of place against whatever blights may sweep across the land will we prevent the forlorn fate of so many older neighborhoods around the country.

Arm in arm, my mother and I continued our slow walk around the block, cautiously cool and optimistic beneath the sheltering arms of our elegant elms. Just then, the final couplet of Shelley's "Ozymandias" came back to me. The poem ends:

> *Round the decay*
> *Of that colossal wreck, boundless and bare,*
> *The lone and level sands stretch far away.*

On Saturday the Urban Coyote Stayed Home

(February 1985)

Today, the last Saturday in January 1985, is the coldest day of the year. Of the decade, some say. Ninety below wind-chill in northern Minnesota, seventy below in the nearby wind tunnels of downtown Minneapolis. Don't leave home for any reason whatsoever, advise the avuncular voices of WCCO radio, our neighbor to the Great Northwest. What sensible advice, I say to myself. I'm taking it. This is one Saturday the Urban Coyote stays home.

Normally, Saturday represents my opportunity to try to get everything done that has ever been put off, which in my case is a lot.

Not this frigid Saturday. I don't dare take back the Christmas shopping mistakes. No way can I visit my neighbors up and down the block whom I have not seen nearly enough of these last few winter months. It's impossible to jog or ski to get the physical exercise I so badly need. It's way too cold to take the kids to the neighborhood shopping center to smell the gourmet chocolate chip cookies and the scented candles. Forget any frenzied last-minute runs to the hardware store to buy a snow rake, to the auto store for replacement jumper cables, to the library with the kids to take back the stack of overdue books and check out new ones, or to the office for a few quiet hours digging out the "In" basket.

What will I do instead? Out the bedroom window, nasty straight-line winds make the streetlight plunge and dip. Occasionally a car aches by on the street. A solitary humanoid crunches frozen snow in thick robot boots. A jet thunders overhead, somehow much louder in thin, icy air.

I notice frost on the inside of several windows. Our daughter's bedroom window is entirely opaque with it. All right, so I refused to risk my life last fall to put up that particular storm window because the borrowed ladder was so unstable. Ha ha, can't do anything about it now. And our bedroom window has a frostbitten bottom because the storm window isn't closed perfectly. So I'm sloppy, I don't care, not today. As for the window for which I built a storm window last year but never got around to putting it up because I was going to paint it first . . . too late now.

I am climbing into bed. I am pulling up the covers. I am gathering unread magazines around me of nearly infinite variety and vintage. I'm having myself a read. Ahhh.

And a nap. Ahhh.

And now it's five o'clock. And it's still Saturday. And I am going to do something I have never done before. I'm going to listen to an entire broadcast, the full two hours, of *A Prairie Home Companion*. Ahhh.

On "normal" Saturdays I manage to catch only snatches of the show while insanely wrapping up Saturday errands. Invariably I am pulling into the Rex Hardware parking lot just before closing as Garrison Keillor's monologue begins, "Well, it's been a quiet week in Lake Wobegon, my hometown...," and I'm scrambling to get the baby out of the car but first get her mittens on and the scarf over her head and now run into the store and grab the paint and fuses and rope and wire and stand in line and finally pay and forget the stuff and grab the kid or grab the stuff and forget the kid and run back out to the car and hear maybe a couple of good lines but miss the gist of the story.

Not today. Today I am snug in bed. All the four children are temporarily subdued by runny winter colds. Mrs. Coyote has declared dinner catch-as-catch-can. I can listen to it all. And I do.

I lie in bed, moving only enough to laugh out loud or sing along. I warm up with Jean Redpath's reedy Scottish soprano singing about food from *Roget's Thesaurus* and the Canadian Brass Ensemble playing Bach's little fugue in some key or other followed by a tuba rag. Then Greg Brown sings his mournful deep bass melodies and another Scottish group does a positively funky bagpipe number, followed by the Department of Folksong's zany rounds. And Garrison's parody advertisements. And finally his monologue. His story. His sermon.

It's about Harold Starr, editor of the community newspaper of the same name if probably not the same spelling, and how Harold, due to a run of bad luck, has developed a nasty mood that encourages him to sound off against Minnesota in general and Lake Wobegon in particular in his weekly editorial. Which is unusual for Harold.

Harold opines that "there's a lot too much talk about 'quality of life' up here...." And Garrison himself gets into the act, telling people who have moved away from small towns but who are nostalgic and don't want anything to change back there, Garrison tells them, well, to "shove it." It's an instructive story. Clearly, however, Minnesota's bad weather is affecting moods behind the story as well as inside it.

But not in my bed. Not this Saturday. Not during this Minnesota winter, bad as this day is. The theater of seasons, like dramas in other theaters, really plays out inside the heads of the audience. My head is in the right spot. Right on the pillow, surrounded by warm magazines and warming airwaves.

When you're in the right spot, enjoying warmth and peace and quiet, then all the neighborhood women are strong, all the men are good-looking and all the children are above average, even your own. And the nastiest of weather brings you right back home where you belong.

Coyote Circles at Honeywell

(May 1986)

Our thirteen-year-old son asked me if I could drop him off at Honeywell's corporate headquarters on my way to work. With his friend Chris. At 6:30 in the morning.

Sure, I said, no problem. Of course, it's a school day so we usually don't have friends sleep over, so what will Chris be doing here? And I usually don't drive anywhere near Honeywell headquarters on my way to work. And of course I am not at all startled by the assertion that the lad wants to be somewhere at 6:30 in the morning. Not a bit.

Young man, I asserted, there is an alien occupying your body! No, he said, Chris and I want to go to the Honeywell Protest.

Ahhhh, I said, the Honeywell Project protest. Are you sure? I mean, we are talking 6:30 a.m.?

Sure, he said. They make bombs that kill lots of people. I thought that they made nuclear bombs, but Mom said that they only make small bombs. Still, I don't think that they ought to make any bombs, and I don't think that Reagan should have bombed Libya, either, and aside from that I'm not so sure what I think but Chris' parents go to lots of protests and I want to go to this one.

Listening to his eager voice, visions from my own past, shed now like an old snake skin, came crawling back to me.

Sixteen years ago I stood outside the entrance to the corporate headquarters of Honeywell in Minneapolis. Vietnam War protests raged all around the country. An infant group named the Honeywell Project had decided that the way to concentrate people's anger against the war was to focus pressure on local institutions. The closest local institution in Minnesota doing the Pentagon's business was Honeywell, the manufacturer of anti-personnel bombs that killed efficiently and indiscriminately.

Full of righteousness and outrage over a war I believed a tragic mistake, I drove to Honeywell's corporate offices near downtown Minneapolis. There I joined hundreds of other like-minded souls milling in front of the main entrance. Our objective was to challenge Honeywell's officers during the annual stockholders' meeting.

The protest was organized by Marv Davidov, a prodigious local organizer of antiwar activities. Protesters were handed pieces of paper indicating that we had legal voting rights for one share of Honeywell stock and therefore had the right to attend the meeting. Then we were instructed by bullhorn to approach the front door, now flanked by dozens of uniformed police officers, apparently edgy. Honeywell management had ordered that only those with valid proxies could enter the building. People jammed up against the door while nervous guards checked credentials. Chanting, shouting and pushing escalated. Tempers flared. The front door collapsed into shards of glass. Mayhem followed. Somehow I ended up inside the building and eventually reached the stockholders' meeting room. I stood against the wall while numerous angry protesters hurled bitter questions at the presiding Chairman of the Board Jim Binger, a tall, white-haired man. The atmosphere crackled with dangerous electricity. Realizing he could no longer control events, Binger declared that the proxy votes supported management positions and abruptly adjourned the meeting. As he left the stage scuffles broke out around the room.

I emerged from the building dazed and disoriented. Outside, tear gas laced the air. Police were dragging several protesters off toward squad cars. Other protesters ran in crazy circles. As the arrested ones were shoved into squad cars, I was both afraid for myself and envious of their conviction.

I drove home slowly, back to my wife, two children and teaching job, wondering what had just happened. I wasn't sure. But I felt that at least I had taken action. At least there was movement.

Movement. For several years, my wife and I had been

part of what was then called The Movement, a loose amalgam of grass-roots groups created to oppose the war in Viet Nam but expanded into a broad agenda for social change. We took our first son to Viet Nam war protests in his baby carriage, his sunbonnet festooned with protest buttons. By the time of the first Honeywell protest, we had marched and held hands in circles many times, singing "We Shall Overcome" over and over again. We were practiced protesters.

Today I am sixteen years out of practice. The young father who stood dazed, confused, fearful and angry among the police and tear gas outside Honeywell's corporate offices is now employed in corporate America and enjoying himself. In addition, I've learned that Honeywell is an exceptional corporate citizen. It maintains offices in the inner city, paradoxically making itself an easy target for just the kind of protests it has sustained nearly every year since the first one. It is an unusually generous corporation in assisting nonprofit organizations, not only with money but also with time and corporate commitment.

Finally, at 41 years old I see an individual corporation as an inappropriate target for anti-war protests. The Pentagon orders the bombs and orders them dropped, and the Pentagon works for elected officials. Honeywell provides what the Pentagon orders, not the other way around. The appropriate place to apply public pressure, therefore, is on politicians, not corporations. So today I'm active in political campaigns, local and national. That's where the real action is, I now believe.

Which is why I no longer march in circles with the Honeywell Project. It is a fine occasion for personal statements of individual commitment, but it seems to me to accomplish little to slow war or stop production of anti-personnel weapons in the world.

Clearly, if Honeywell and the Honeywell Project haven't changed much in sixteen years, I certainly have. I have become the pragmatic fuddy-duddy my youthful protesting self warned me against.

Yet there I was, parked in the Honeywell parking lot, the latest annual anti-war protest assembled right in front of me. The spring sky was already a high blue, the air clean and warm, the flowers beginning to germinate near the milling feet of the gathered protesters and police officers, many now good friends in what has become an annual spring ritual. Across from the main corporate entrance a ring of peace-loving people sang "We Shall Overcome." As I listened, singing along in my mind, my son opened the back door of the car and he and Chris jumped out and jogged over to join the group. I waved but they didn't look back.

As I watched them disappear into the crowd, I heard a familiar voice over the bullhorn offering the protesters their instructions in the practice of civil disobedience. Marv Davidov! He's still organizing his Project, still keeping himself and his testament alive after sixteen years, while some of his original comrades have fallen into child-rearing, corporations and pragmatism. Well, good for him. Keep the faith, brother.

The group enfolded my son and Chris arm in arm as they walked and chanted slowly in concentric circles, basking in the inner glow of solidarity. They cheered their technical achievement of keeping concentric circles turning. The cheer made me chuckle, here in front of the headquarters of a company whose spinning gyroscopes bring jetliners safely into airports in zero visibility.

Then I heard Marv Davidov squawk over the bullhorn: "Who is prepared to commit civil disobedience? Who will cross the police line and get arrested?" I glanced at the police van waiting nearby, its back door open and waiting, the officers relaxed and smiling.

The singing stopped, and members of the circle clasped hands in silence. I felt the weight of that silence in my neck and shoulders. Would my life be different had I stepped over that line sixteen years ago? Would my son step over today?

Several seasoned protesters, white-haired and wrapped in dignity, took a step. Just then a uniformed policeman leaned into my car window. Sorry sir, he said in a friendly tone, you'll have to leave now. No idling here any longer. Not today. Yes, officer, I said.

I slowly drove out of the Honeywell parking lot and headed south on the freeway toward my corporate office. Projects with deadlines were waiting for me to step forward and make decisions.

But thinking about that day today, I might have better served the universe by turning off the freeway into a field of emerging flowers, lying down on my back in the spring sun and howling at the resurrection and the light, the birth and rebirth of the earth, and of ourselves.

The State Fair Is Worth Every Penny

(September 1986)

Ever summer since we moved to Minnesota, I've taken a gaggle of children to the State Fair in St. Paul. Country people do their city cousins an immense favor by bringing their work right to us. We know you are busy people, they say, moving so fast you line up at drive-thru windows. If you visit the country at all you probably just pass through hurrying to stake your claim to peace and quiet by a northern lake or under a white pine. So we'll bring the country to you. Here, see and smell and touch what we do. The experience will refresh your ancestral memories of the land, of animals, of husbandry.

And so it does. If you can find parking.

This year I found myself stuck in the left lane in sight of the fairgrounds with "no left turn" signs stretching over the horizon. It looked bad. An illegal U-turn later, I was in luck. I found a spot on a lawn only a few blocks from the State Fair's southeast entrance, my favorite. Of course, I had to pay $5 for the privilege, but it was worth it. Ever since they sighted the Ferris wheel, my four-year-old daughter and eight-year-old niece visiting from New York were so anxious they were climbing out the windows. So the rotund woman with the hand-lettered "parking" sign waving her cane appeared to me not as a gouger from Hell but as an angel of mercy.

Now was the time for my annual State Fair lecture, perfected since we first brought the older children here a decade ago. OK, kids, there are certain things we must do, and others we must not. We will not, for example, go on rides. Except the merry-go-round. The merry-go-round is OK. But nothing else. Rides are rip-offs that make you sick. OK?

Here are things we must do. Touch all the farm animals and see all the wild animals and fish at the Department of Natural Resources exhibit. And overeat. Any questions?

No questions. They were already running toward the entrance.

We walked right past the first opportunity for overeating, the Dairy Building, where the world's finest strawberry malts are served. At ten in the morning the place was already mobbed. "We'll come back later, but this is a must," said Dad, beginning to drool.

There was no line at the cotton candy stand. "This is a must," said my youngest daughter. OK, OK. I bought one. Three steps later we threw it in the nearest trash barrel. Way too sweet. Have to try one next year though.

What's that, a new ride? A white water raft ride? Say, that looks like fun. Shall we? OK, we're in. Hey, this is fun. Sorry you got all wet, kids. But, take it from the Old Man, rafting is fun. Shall we do it again?

Instead we went looking for bunnies. We found chickens. The poultry building echoed with cock-a-doodle-doos from strutting punk rock roosters. The sound, plus the pungency of chicken excrement, pushed us right into the silent bunnies, satin soft, some with ears large as slippers.

In the next building we learned humility. Draft horses— huge Clydesdales, Belgians and Percherons—stomped and snorted. These herbivore four-wheel-drive tractors amazed us with their power and grace. The kids reached out and touched the softest skin on earth, a horse's nose, then watched a farrier nail a horseshoe. We petted goats and stuck our fingers up to our knuckles into the oily wool of sheep. We watched teenaged boys rub down a Clydesdale's fetlocks with sawdust and teenaged girls hose down their prize Holsteins and Guernseys. We watched sheep getting a haircut and shampoo.

We emerged from the dusty barns ravenously hungry. Three hot ears of corn with fresh butter and salt and pepper, please. And three Cokes.

Licking buttery fingers, we entered the Swine Building

just as the "FFA Swine Show Showmanship Contest" began. We jumped into the stands and watched adolescent men and women enter the ring, each shepherding a single Duroc, Hampshire, Yorkshire, or Poland China. Each youth guided his charge with a small stick or whip.

The judge, a wiry FFA elder, addressed the contestants and, over their heads, the city slickers in the audience about what he intended to consider. "The issue here is showmanship—not so much of the hog as the shower. You want to keep good eye contact, keep the hog ranging, don't get too close to the judge."

The contest began. There was plenty of eye contact as the kids watched the judge intently while crouching over their hogs and flicking them this way and that with their sticks.

An older farmer sitting in front of us tilted back his head in reverie. "Try to get those suckers up a loading chute," he said with a tobacco-stained smile, eyes filled with nostalgia. "Sometimes they go up just fine. But I remember the day I was loading forty-five of 'em. Had to carry each one up the chute. All the way," he chuckled out loud. Clearly herding pigs is not just an academic exercise.

The judge selected five finalists and lectured them again.

"Your business should be focused in the ring," the judge said. "This is a business. Showmanship is an indication of your attitude. Now I want you to guide your pig back and forth between these chairs I've set up. Then pen them. OK, let's go."

Before it was over my niece guessed which boy would be the winner. The lad moved like a crab in his attentive crouch while smoothly guiding his young pink and black Duroc. The judge, a Ph.D. at the University, agreed with my niece from New York City.

The winner, from tiny Glencoe, Minnesota, wore blue

jeans and a white shirt. His blond hair was cut short at the top and long at the back in the latest proto-punk fashion, but he demonstrated a heck of a business attitude.

It was a sensational pig show and we applauded wildly, but it inspired a bit of envy in this city dweller. There is, I thought, something authentic and serious about the raising and judging of pigs. I'm not sure I'll increase my family's ration of pork to keep this boy from Glencoe, Minnesota on his farm. But I'm not sure I won't, either.

Leaving the pig judging area, we admired a sow nursing thirteen piglets. There we greeted a friend from the neighborhood herding his own brood of children and foster children. They ogled the pig family with us.

Then we ran over to the sign declaring this year's winner of the "Minnesota's Largest Boar contest!" The four and one-half year-old Spotted boar raised by the Rodney Skalbeck family of Sacred Heart, Minnesota weighed 1,020 pounds!

A 1,020-pound pig? Before you digest the weight of that sentence, consider this. The largest draft horses weigh 2,300 pounds, the largest bulls 2,000 pounds. The draft horses stand six feet tall, the bulls five feet. This boar walks six inches off the floor. My hat is off to the Rodney Skalbeck family of Sacred Heart, Minnesota. I sure hope they don't have to carry him up the chute.

Time to stock up at the green pepper stand and strawberry shortcake stand. Three of everything, please. And a stop at the beer stand. One large please. Then on to the Midway.

There's the merry-go-round. OK, OK, I said, but I have to buy coupons first. At the coupon window, I was forearmed by memories of past years' coupon fiascoes. No way was I going to be caught up in the old ten dollars for thirty coupons scam. No way. Purchasing a book saved fifty cents per ten dollars worth of rides, but since we were only going on the merry-go-round, we didn't need the extra tickets.

So I outfoxed the hucksters. I bought only enough coupons for two children and one adult for one ride. Nine coupons later, we were on the merry-go-round, me going around and around smiling weakly at the crowd, half my beer sloshing in my hand, the other half sloshing in my stomach.

Bumper cars? I didn't know they had bumper cars at the Fair. Back to the coupon booth. Five coupons later, my niece was riding the bumper cars, driving insanely as we watched. Bumper cars may be the nail in the coffin of male domination. Over half the drivers in this electric flotilla were female, all with determined expressions on their faces, delighting in male bashing.

Tilt-A-Whirl? Hey, we've gotta do the Tilt-A-Whirl. Back to the coupon booth. Nine coupons later, we stepped into the half-saucers. OK, said the attendant, everybody ready to get sick? My empty beer cup crumpled in my hand.

Wait a minute! Could that really be the World's Smallest Horse, so small a baby can ride it? Fed by only a cupful of water and a handful of grain? Back to the booth. Nine tickets later, we were peering down onto a very small horse indeed, about the size of a collie, but one instantly recognizable as a standard miniature breed. There are thousands of these horses around the country. "What a rip-off," we complained to each other as we exited.

The attendant saw me writing something in my notebook and came over to offer helpful information. "They live to be six, then they die after that," he said. "Say, this ain't for no TV show, is it? I ain't for no TV show. Then we'd lose business." I'll say.

Next I saw posters for "The Fattest Man in the World, Fat Albert. 861 pounds. 22 pounds at birth. *Guinness Book* of *World Records*. 9-foot waistline. Size 20 shoe." Fascinating, but we passed, finally hip to the hype. We noted that the sign didn't say Fat Albert is *in* the *Guinness Book of World Records*.

But the Ferris wheel? We have to do the Ferris wheel. Back to the booth. Fifteen coupons later, we were climbing one hundred feet over the Minnesota State Fair. Clumps of white clouds floated like cotton candy over us, the fair grounds full of brightly colored gummi bear humans below. So what if we had to look at the painting of Fat Albert's navel twenty times as the wheel circled? It was worth every coupon. As we scratched the sky, we saw the high-rises and neighborhoods and lakes and farms of Minnesota radiate out from its festival heart.

Still high from spinning we exited the Midway past the last grinning hucksters and immediately downed three pronto pups and a sack of greasy donuts made fresh right outside the gate. As for the strawberry malts from the Dairy Building, they were the best ever, in spite of the long wait in line to get them.

Before leaving the fairgrounds for home, we walked through the wild animal exhibit in the Department of Natural Resources Building. We particularly noted the coyote, *canis latrans*, sleeping with his tail over his eyes. We read that Coyotes have expanded their range throughout the state nearly to the suburban perimeter of the Twin Cities. This one must be dreaming of all the food he sees here. Will there soon be urban coyotes as well?

Outside, we leaned over the large fishpond. We marveled at our indigenous underwater neighbors cruising in the fresh water. Several Mississippi River paddlefish were as big as small sharks. A massive catfish swam below us with twenty-nine cents balanced on his broad forehead—nine pennies, two nickels and one dime thrown there by youthful well-wishers. Each of us tried our luck. Our three copper pennies flashed in the sun like Ferris wheels, then fluttered through the clear water to settle on the pond bottom. We thought we saw the catfish smile.

At the Minnesota State Fair even the fish take cash. The celebration of statewide community is worth every penny.

Pets—What a Fine Idea

(April 1987)

The family just returned from a weekend trip to find our soft, purring cat awaiting us on our front doorstep. He emerged from under the arbor vitae, eyes groggy with sleep.

My five-year-old daughter rushed up to "kitty" in delight, picked him up, hugged him and swore her love. Then she carried him like an old dishrag up the porch and into the house and immediately forced him into an old doll dress, much too small, berating him for trying to get away. "No, kitty, no!"

The rest of us entered the empty house. Well, not quite empty. Over in the corner three birds looked at us mournfully. A silent canary. A biting conure (a small, aggressive parrot). A loud cockatiel.

Where did these unrelated beasts come from? I had vowed never to have pets. Four children are more than enough responsibility, and I can at least eat their leftovers.

It all began with the cat, once only a mournful stray kitten. My eldest daughter adopted him twelve years ago when he appeared at the back door. Over parental protestations, she gave him milk. That was that.

He insinuated himself into our daily lives. First he slept outside. Then on the back porch. Then inside. Then in some-one's bed. Then on someone's head.

Defeated, I vowed at least that I would never buy pet food, an insult to a poorly fed world population (the very idea of pet food sold in stores absolutely cracks up visitors from China, confirming their incredulity at our culture of excess). He would only get table scraps, when and where we felt like it. Finally, as he appeared to be starving because someone would forget to feed him, I broke down and bought a bag of cat food, the dry stuff, sort of cat bran flakes. Ten years later, our recycling container is full of empty cans of Cat Filet Mignon, Cat Paté, Cat Terrine, Cat Salmon.

Our house is also a bit poorer in other ways.

Cat markings. Hundreds of cats have pissed on our front porch. Our cat has already pissed on our new refrigerator. Welcome.

Cat prints walk over the car, the tub, the toilet, the sink, the ceiling.

Cat fights. I did not grow up with cats. I learned of them from old Sunday comics with pictures of people throwing shoes out of windows to silence howling cats. How quaint, I thought. Now we throw shoes, books, chairs, bureaus.

Sleeplessness. Somebody has to put the beast out at night. "Somebody" always fails. Our sleep is routinely punctuated by the sound of purring and the sensation of fur in our nostrils. Outside he goes. Then he needs to get back in. So it goes throughout the night while the children sleep.

Not to mention shredded upholstery, only the best stuff.

As I write this, in the early morning quiet before work, the affectionate cat has just come in from the cold. He is purring like an electromagnetic device. He exercises his claws against my sport coat. He strolls up onto the kitchen table. He stands between my face and my notebook. I can't see a thing, but I can feel his fuzz in my nostrils. Could he possibly want something?

Of course he wants something. Food. He will not stop breaking my concentration until I feed him. I feed him.

The Stone Age sounds of the Fred Flintstone family emerge suddenly from the living room accompanied by the laughter of the five-year-old who has sneaked downstairs to catch early morning cartoons. Over the noise of the TV, the cockatiel begins his morning song. "Whoop, whoop, whoop," he shrills continuously, celebrating the sunrise. "Be quiet," shouts my daughter, the pet lover. "Be quiet. Be quiet."

The bird joined our family like this.

My twelve-year-old son badgered us for a parrot for over a year. He swore he would feed it, change its cage weekly, clip its wings and toenails. I knew these were lies – I was not born yesterday. But I was weak. My father had just died, and I felt a sense of loss. A parrot (a conure, it turned out) came home with us from the pet store, named Teddy after my father.

That was years ago. Since then a pair of cockatiels joined the party. My son needed to breed them—an educational project, he said, just like the one at school. Instead, the female died after six months of his erratic care. Stiff and dead. We made him bury it, which made him moan unhappily. The male cockatiel was more unhappy, howling mournfully night and day for weeks from my son's room.

Educational? Definitely. Sadness at death knows no bounds. And after a while life goes on.

Rabbits and finches and turtles and fish. They all ended in the garden.

In some ways gerbils were our most successful pet. I spent

weeks in the basement building a miniature Cape Cod cottage for them, with a spiral staircase and a unique hinged roof for easy cage cleaning. It was a masterpiece of gerbilaceous architecture. Unfortunately the cat discovered the access. The gerbils disappeared or dropped dead, simply scared to death. That's OK. The kids had lost interest.

But not me. Gerbils and their fellow pets taught me the meaning of life. With no apologies to William Blake and his poem "The Tyger," I offer the following lines:

Gyrbyl, Gyrbyl, Scratching Late

> *Gyrbyl, gyrbyl, scratching late*
> *in the cages of the night,*
> *which of my irresponsible children*
> *failed to feed thee once again?*
>
> *Gyrbyl, gyrbyl, I created you,*
> *brought you home one pleasant birthday.*
> *I brought no intent of slaughter,*
> *only rules on food and water.*
>
> *Gyrbyl, gyrbyl, I maintained you,*
> *brought you paper tubes to run through,*
> *built a cage of wood and wire,*
> *let you out when kids were in school.*
>
> *Gyrbyl, now that you're dead and gone,*
> *in your cage, stiff, cold as stone,*
> *I don't cry, but this I learn:*
> *to play God is to be alone.*

Part One

Kids — What a Fine Idea

(May 1987)

Kids—what a fine idea. Conceived as an insurance policy for their parents' old age, children tend to the hunting, gathering and dusting when parents become too old, too stiff, too wise. Their parents, meanwhile, finally get to lie around dispensing the wisdom they earned with every white hair, bleeding ulcer, broken limb and stupid mistake. Old age is the chance to relax, show off, teach the next generation the hard won ABC's of life.

What went wrong?

In several important areas, my children already know far more than I do. In the new ABC's of adolescent life—sex, drugs and rock 'n' roll—there is very little I know and even less that they don't know.

SEX. When I was growing up, "sex" was an underground concept. If it was mentioned at all, it was in the back pages of sleazy magazines that only existed in somebody else's uncle's brother's friend's hunting cabin Up North somewhere.

In day-to-day living, sex had no vocabulary whatsoever. Around my house, parents whispered the word "pregnant."

The pulp magazine topic of the day, and the crucial concept in relationships, was *Romance*. Romance, not sex, was the necessary fantasy, and one I still believe far more compelling—something that lasts for decades, not hours or minutes.

About sex we all had to learn the hard way, fumbling around in the dark.

Certainly this is not the best way to learn about one of

the six central facts of life (the others are birth, death, work, family and community). So thirty years or so ago, my generation decreed: Let there be light.

Today sex is a public obsession. A titillating whine rises from innumerable babbling talk shows on TV and radio and from the covers of magazines at our local drugstore. Sex stares us in the face from passing bus billboards and behind the counter at the video store.

My children know more about sex than I do. Name the junior high kid today who can't carry on a fully informed conversation on "the many faces of transvestitism."

Were the blind, deaf and dumb old days better or merely benighted? Are the sex-drenched new days enlightened or simply pornographic? I don't know. I do know that I am not a happy camper as a parent lost in this sexual swamp without new social signposts to help guide me through.

DRUGS. When I was growing up, drugs consisted of Bayer aspirin and Milk of Magnesia. Both were more or less abhorred and certainly resisted to the last breath.

Now junior high kids announce at the dinner table, "I'm never going to use crack, and certainly not ice or 'ludes. So what are you worried about?"

So who said I was worried? But what is ice? What are 'ludes?

ROCK 'N' ROLL. Music has become a subversive force between generations. There are whole radio stations of music that defy description by an adult. Some of it may be only radio interference. Some of it may actually have melody.

The point is, parents know nothing about this stuff. How can I guide my children through the thorn patch of adolescence with any credibility if I can't be certain that Iron Maiden is "punk" or "heavy metal"? And by the way, what is "heavy metal"?

As a parent, not to mention as an experienced human being over 40, I am the one who is supposed to be giving out advice and wisdom, yet I am ignorant of the new ABC's.

So I set myself to grumbling out loud about the pervasiveness of sex, drugs and rock n' roll. Sure music is wonderful and important, but a Walkman on the head while walking to school or walking in the woods? When can a child really listen, think and imagine? Sure, sex is important, but on nearly every TV show and magazine cover?

And drugs. Cocaine has become as easy to get as after-school ice cream. Whatever happened to pencil-shaving cigarettes?

My five-year-old daughter just got her first bicycle. She is enthralled and wants to ride everywhere. I take her around the block every evening after work, her training wheels spinning with excitement and accomplishment.

Is this the last time I can teach her anything? Next year she'll be tall enough to see over the video store counter past *Dumbo* to *Debbie Does Dallas*, past *Sheera, Princess of Power* to *The Shame of Peaches and Cream.* And she will begin to know more than I am able to tell her.

She will stroll back into the street holding my hand, a fairy tale video tucked firmly under her arm. We will bump headlong into aggressive music thumping from passing cars and Calvin Klein bus billboards displaying anorexic adolescents in near-pornographic poses.

When can I ever teach her the facts of life I do know something about—birth, death, work, family, community? Such stories don't make headlines, not to mention radio station babble, but make every day alive, necessary and sometimes ecstatic.

It was King Lear who found it "sharper than a serpent's tooth to have a thankless child." Today's adults struggle against a thankless culture where children learn everything they think they need to know from screaming FM radio dee-jays, street pushers and the scenery behind the counter at the video store.

Like Lear, I am less than enthusiastic to have become a living fossil whose perceived knowledge is as up-to-date as stone axes, whose assistance on the path of modern life is as relevant as buried bones.

Memorial Day and Other Rituals

(June 1987)

The small Wisconsin town where I grew up always held a big Memorial Day parade on the main street. Squadrons of Cub Scouts, Brownies, Girl Scouts, Sea Scouts, Explorer Scouts, Legionnaires, members of Auxiliary This and Club That marshalled themselves into semi-straight lines and marched to the rhythm of drum and bugle corps like some lurching surge of musical army ants. The parade ended at the town center, an intersection where the highway bridged the river that flowed through a paper mill and over a dam. A twenty-one gun salute puffed out over the bridge while buglers played the soulful lamentations of taps in the background.

As the flag marched by, my father would grab my shoulders from behind in his strong grip and remind me in my ear that my grandfather always cried when the flag went by. My father's eyes were streaming too. So were mine.

My family, three generations deep and numerous cousins wide in that town, followed up the parade with a trip to the family cemetery plot atop a bluff a mile upriver from downtown. Oak and hickory and cottonwood leaves flashed bright new growth over the water silted red with clay. We would hold hands in a circle around the graves of departed parents and grandparents and uncles and aunts, improvising prayers and telling family stories. Tears would run again down my father's cheeks. Then we children would wander among the neighboring gravestones, the names inscribed there as familiar to us as the families in the neighborhood where we lived together.

Even as I grew older and detested dressing up in a suit or uniform, not to mention going places with my family and not my friends, I never resented those Memorial Days. As an adult, observing Memorial Day pass in a city far away from that riverbank, I deeply miss the warm pressure of the generations in my hands, the flash of the cottonwood, those familiar headstones and that river of continuity.

It was a ritual that literally touched me. Within its warm preserve, I found the space to let the most unsettling questions of birth and death and community dissolve into the blood of familiarity and larger consequence.

Boy, do I ever need that feeling now.

This Memorial Day weekend, the life of the Urban Coyote is circumscribed by chaos. The house is chock-full of children. Why did we have so many? The kitchen and a bedroom are being remodeled. What were we thinking of? Big Scary Problems cloud the political horizon. What is a citizen to do?

Our eldest son, The Big Guy, just returned from college. That's exciting except his bedroom is currently occupied by his sister because the contractor is sheetrocking her room so he is sleeping on the screen porch couch and leaves the door open which becomes a superhighway for the spring bottle flies who buzz around the house day and night like B-52's. Of course he has piled all his worldly belongings—a laundry bag full of miscellaneous clothing, three hundred meticulously catalogued audio tapes and a stereo—in the middle of the living room, because there is no place else to put them. Which no one notices after a few days because they become covered with a white silt of sheetrock dust like the rest of the house. Including the dirty dishes, which are balanced miraculously on the edge of the tiny bathroom sink because the old kitchen sink is being replaced so now when the children wash their hands they have to be extra careful to avoid washing the dishes, which they somehow manage.

Today the dishes finally teeter because the five-year-old is playing hopscotch in the sheetrock dust and trips and lands hard on her butt and howls with pain at exactly the same moment that her fifteen-year-old brother arrives home late for lunch again with a spectacular skateboard airborne wheelie that might have wowed the crowds on Venice Beach in LA but for one slight miscalculation regarding a geranium planter on the front porch. At which point the seventeen-year-old sister shrieks that she can't study for final examinations with all these screaming and crashing bozos in the house and storms off for a vengeful afternoon of shopping at Calhoun Square, slamming the door hard behind her. At which sound the Missus, laboring in her home office under a hair-raising deadline, turns the locks with a calm indication that she will not come out, ever. At which point I come home. And the dishes fall.

Decisions, decisions. Pick up the shards or put out the fire in the toaster? Clean the fuming kitty litter or feed the starving bird? How can the schools have so many different programs? How can children be so different and need so many different programs? And kitchen tile. How can there be so many different kinds of kitchen tile? Our house is littered with sample blocks of granite, chips of marble, hunks of terra cotta and ribbons of glazed ceramic. Hey, it's only a kitchen. What ever happened to white? OK, white it is. Do we want white white or buff white? Do we want one inch tiles or two, four inch or eight? Square or octagonal?

But why worry about such small inconveniences? The evening news reports an impending international economic collapse while politicians fall like comets and ecologists notice a lack of rain this year and too much rain last year. Wealthy businessmen threaten to leave Minnesota because of our "oppressive" tax climate while international bureaucrats forbid thousands of sick and starving Asian and African refugees from leaving sick and stifling refugee camps.

That was Saturday. On Sunday, I sat alone in church.

It had been a long time, but there I was, pew to pew with the regulars. I needed some place to rest, to clear my head, to think, to not think, to find peace. Far from the riverbank of my youth, far from those generations spread around me, I found a place where a powerful river still flows.

Weekly religious services. Memorial Day parades. All such rituals give meaning and context to the chaos of the day-to-day. In a society that so worships individuality and variety, communal sameness provides a healing benediction. No society needs it more than modern America, yet no society so fears it, throws it off, distrusts it.

We need to return ritual to its rightful place. To stand

together holding hands as memories and stories run from the elders to the young, who begin to feel through touch the impression of their own true significance. And generations feel together the peace of the river as the spring trees bloom.

Reading Groups: The Novel

(September 1987)

When Faulkner was asked what were the three greatest novels ever written, he responded *Anna Karenina, Anna Karenina, Anna Karenina*. At 46 years old, I still haven't read any of Faulkner's top three selections. What I need is a reading group. I know because I recently joined one.

My group began—as most probably do—as the inspiration of a friend that hit the rest of us just at the moment we realized we might never again find the time to read a novel in its entirety, not to mention a "good" novel.

The grouping was serendipitous—a rare bookseller, a librarian ex-nun, a lawyer, a business executive, a marketing communications consultant (me). Our only common bond was the desire to read and discuss good books.

Our first meeting took place early one Saturday morning at a small cafe with a reputation for good breakfasts and a more or less functional espresso machine. Since the machine belched out excellently frothed au laits that day, our discussion seemed to spark. We agreed to continue to meet at the restaurant on an irregular basis depending upon the length of the book under discussion. We also agreed that we would read only novels, a decision that caused the lawyer to grumble, then quietly drop out (turned out he's a biography man), although another member joined later (a cartoonist with a penchant for Thomas Hardy).

I was chosen to inflict upon the group the first selection. As I am prone to strange enthusiasms myself, I foolishly picked my favorite book of prose, *The Life and Opinions of Tristram Shandy, Gent.* by Lawrence Sterne.

Reading groups beware, this was a mistake! *Tristram Shandy* nearly suffocated our reading group in its crib.

It is a wildly eccentric book, with random pages blank or solid black, others with type skidding down the page edge like a lightning bolt, the plot nearly impossible to follow. I love it.

But sensing in the following weeks a growing frustration within the group, I drafted written guidelines designed to make the book less maddening. Unfortunately for my readers, I finished the "Guide to the maddening plot convolutions of *Tristram Shandy, Gent.*" the day of the scheduled discussion, not before. The damage was done. Eyeballs were rolling.

Again, however, the au laits frothed. We added toast and omelets and everyone's outlook improved. My fellow group members decided not to kill me after all. We decided to try again.

The remainder of the year we discussed a parade of interesting works, including *Moby Dick* (have *you* actually read *all* the chapters?) and Toni Morrison's splendid *Beloved*.

The group ended our first year's meetings in June with a tasty discussion of Flaubert's *Madame Bovary* and an enthusiastic pledge to gather again in September. What book should we read over the summer?

An aside on our method of choosing works, about which groups apparently differ. We adopted the timeless and proven schoolyard system: The taking of turns. However, mindful of the *Tristram Shandy* experience, we included a silent caveat that the choice should inspire a more or less enthusiastic consensus. Here is where trouble can start.

After much tantalizing coffee talk of taking on James Joyce's *Ulysses* (we decided not to ruin our summer), I was not pleased to hear our sole woman member's stubbornly firm choice: George Eliot's *Middlemarch*. What? Nearly eight hundred pages of mid-nineteenth century English small town life, written by a female who adopted a male pseudonym? That seemed to me every bit a torture equal to tangling with Joyce's book-length sentences. I growled my assent, since it was her turn, choosing to suppress my suspicion that this was the mustiest of tomes. Why not *Anna Karenina*? I groaned. She had already read it, but would consider rereading next summer if I wanted.

I write now at summer's end and I'm pleased to report that I enjoyed an exceptional season of reading. A confessed magazine and newspaper addict, I actually completed five shortish books, four of them fiction. For me that is a record, no doubt reflecting time gained by the lower maintenance our children now require.

Of course, none of those books was *Middlemarch*.

Now the last week in August, with the sybaritic pleasures of the State Fair behind me and the September reading group deadline in front of me, I can no longer avoid the monster. The prospect had been so bleak that I conveniently forgot to purchase a copy. Unfortunately, a friend lent me an old volume from his dusty shelf. Dame Fortune would not excuse me so easily.

The children are in bed. I am reaching for the dusty monster. It is heavy. I can hardly lift it. Just as I'd expected, the volume is browned at the edges, the acidic paper consuming itself. My failing eyes can barely make out the eight-point type. The musty pages make me sneeze.

My reading group has made a terrible summer mistake! Shouldn't such a book be reserved for winter, when the alternative is shoveling the driveway or freezing to death? Or did I make a mistake by joining a book group in the first place, adding one more unnecessary obligation to my life? OK, OK, I'll open it.

What's this? Wit? Delight? Romance? Passion? Wisdom? *Middlemarch* is a mid-nineteenth century page-turner, exceedingly clever and, unlike *Tristram Shandy*, coherent as well. I cannot put it down. George Eliot, whatever his or her gender, is a wonderful writer and storyteller. I can face September after all. This is going to be a long, delightful and relaxing read, the perfect summer book.

I have only two questions. Why did I wait until the end of August to begin reading it? And why did I wait until age 46 to join a book group?

My advice to those who love literature: Don't put off a book group. Great coffee, new friendships and *Middlemarch* await. And the possibility will then exist, for you as now for me, that you will not live out your lives without ever having read *Anna Karenina*.

Will the Magic Never End?

(November 1987)

The Minnesota Twins' victory in the 1987 World Series was locked up before the first Series game ever began. When the team returned home the week before, after beating the Detroit Tigers for the American League Championship, the players were ushered into the Metrodome stadium in downtown Minneapolis for a homecoming event. They expected some cheers and a few speeches. What they found were 55,000 blissed-out citizens thanking them for showering honor on our community. They stood there, slack-jawed in amazement. No way they could let this town down.

More amazing yet, Mrs. Coyote was there, the Anti-Fan.

To her, team sports represent the lowest form of peonage. She earns her exercise in the buck-fifty aerobics class down at the elementary school gymnasium. She roller-skates around our neighborhood lakes. She wipes our kitchen counters vigorously. All personal best kind of stuff, not rah rah team cheerleading.

So when she was sucked into the Metrodome with our son and his best friend, cheering wildly to welcome back the American League Champions, Twins mania had claimed its stoutest convert. After that, the St. Louis Cardinals never had a chance.

My conversion was much simpler. I'm a sucker for any religious experience, and community is my religion.

The World Series landed on our city as if Moses and Walt Disney had descended simultaneously. Minnesotans worshipped and were moved, and it was good, and clean, and safe for families. And had a happy ending.

The impenetrable cool of our community was pierced and a whirlwind of emotion escaped.

Yeah! Go Twins!

Everyone felt it. The huge crowd at the World Series victory parade we attended with the kids included a guy walking shakily with an old stick for a cane, wearing a tattered coat, filthy cap and several days' growth of beard. He sported a button on his lapel: "I love the Twins."

Our Number One son, the Big Guy, watched the final game in his college dormitory in Connecticut. When the Twins' victory celebration erupted on the field, he jumped up to exult with his fellow students around him. Not Minnesotans, they were reluctant to partake in his inexpressible joy. Instead, they acted cynical, bored, distant. He returned to his room, depressed. He wanted to share his elation but had no appropriate community around him to share it with.

He tried to phone the family, to touch home base, share the feeling, but couldn't get through. All the telephone circuits to Minnesota were jammed with other members of the Minnesota community calling home, touching base, sharing the feeling.

Two other voices clogging the phone lines that night were those of my wife and eldest daughter, a high school senior. They had left town for a previously scheduled trip to prospect East Coast colleges. Desperate to see the seventh game, they pulled the car off the freeway at a seedy motel in King of Prussia, Pennsylvania and caught the last three innings. They too tried to call home to share the feeling, but couldn't get through.

No matter, I wasn't at home anyway. I was dancing through the downtown streets, our six-year-old daughter riding on my shoulders. She wore her new Twins hat sideways and falling over her eyes. Her T-shirt was decorated with "Win Twins" slogans she had learned to write in kindergarten. Her parka was festooned with Twins buttons.

We wove ecstatically through the streets, high-fiving a thousand other hands. We didn't want the feeling to end. We had attended the seventh game, and we had won.

Wait a minute, you scream! A six-year-old had a ticket for the seventh and final game of the World Series? Yes, she did. Here's her story.

I had purchased four tickets through a friend. I was going. So was our middle son, age fifteen, and his best friend Art. My wife and older daughter were on the aforementioned college road trip, the other son at college.

I was trying to find a sitter for the youngest so that I could offer the extra ticket to any of a thousand friends who in return would do me favors for the rest of my life, when I was visited by a photographer friend, in town to shoot the Series for *Sports Illustrated*. "Take her," he said. "She'll never forget it."

He was right.

I know he was right because after the victory I had lunch with a neighborhood friend I hadn't seen for months. Of course we discussed the World Series and otherwise shared the feeling. He told me he was especially pleased the Twins had won because he loathed the St. Louis Cardinals. Why's that? I asked. He grew up in St. Louis but was a St. Louis Browns fan, therefore a bitter antagonist of the cross-town rival Cardinals.

He said that he became a Browns fan because his parents took him to the World Series in 1948 when he was six years old. He never forgot it.

My friend specifically recalled the Browns' one-armed outfielder. He would catch the ball, drop his glove, grab the ball from the air and fire it in. He batted one-handed. Now that I think of it, said my friend, maybe my lifelong work with the disadvantaged stems from that one-armed vision of transcendence.

What will my six-year-old carry away from her seventh game experience? Will she remember penciling in vital game statistics on the scorecard? Playing tic-tac-toe with me between innings? Wearing earplugs of toilet paper when the crowd noise equaled a jet taking off in the back yard? Snake dancing through euphoric streets at midnight, high-fiving a blissful population?

Perhaps when she grows up she'll become a psychologist with a special research interest in twins. Or a policewoman working crowd control. Perhaps she'll become a religious zealot promoting mass hysteria. Perhaps she'll be stone deaf.

Certainly she will remember the unreality of the last weeks of this particular baseball season– from a community counting magic numbers to a magic community feeling. The Twins, our civic religion, won the Series, and every citizen glows a little more brightly.

PART TWO

CENTER OF THE NEIGHBORHOOD

1988-89

Shared Grief

(January 1988)

I will never forget a voice I heard last summer over National Public Radio. A father was describing his daughter's life slipping away as he held her in his arms. She was the victim of an IRA bombing at a holiday festival.

I remember stopping my car on the side of the road, sharing the grief of that voice three thousand miles away, feeling a mingled sense of rage and helplessness against the slayers of children.

The death of a child is such a violation. I wrote the epitaph for my father in my mind a hundred times before he died at the age of eighty-one. One completes no such exercises for one's children.

This December I heard about Michael.

A friend called to tell us. Michael was at school roughhousing with friends when he collapsed. Some mysterious electrical signal misfired, shutting down his heart. He died immediately. Michael was fifteen years old.

The Shulman family was in shock. The community was stunned. But the invisible networks of both began to weave together.

Michael had played on the first peewee soccer programs ten years ago. Many of us had worked on sports and schools and politics and social issues and park events with Mike's parents, Margaret and Dan, and seen all the five Shulman children grow up.

When I went to the Shulman house on Penn Avenue, I found it filled with neighbors, friends and co-workers. The kitchen and dining room tables were covered with dishes of food. There was a handwritten schedule on the wall indicating what time friends should come by to help serve or clean up, what they should bring, who should pick up new arrivals at the airport.

Community, that invisible network of relationships built through time and involvement, was gathering together around a deep wound to one of its own. It was here to help as needed, to share, and to share the grief.

A few days later a memorial service was held for Michael at his school. The auditorium overflowed with nearly seven hundred people, a breathtaking tribute to the powerful ripples of a young life. The audience included the five communities touched by Michael and his family: family, friends, school, neighborhood, work.

Friends, teachers, coaches and family spoke of their memories of Michael. This was no stiff-upper-lip stuff. These were words wrenched from the vocal chords. This was deep sadness and tears from all the seven hundred. "You all know how hard this is," said Dan.

A few days later I visited the Shulman family again. Margaret and the daughters Amy and Ellen were away. Ten of Michael's school friends were crowded around the kitchen table with Dan and son David, invited over by the Shulmans to talk about Michael. They were sharing memories, part of the process of working at the loss.

A bucket of cookies sat in the middle of the table along with a stack of letters a foot high. A cat jumped up on the table. Mike's cat.

"The hockey team is sewing black armbands on their jerseys," said one of the boys.

"You know what makes me sad," said Dan. "I found a copy of *Huckleberry Finn* in Michael's room. I know now he'll never be able to read that great book." The kids piped up right away. "He did read it, for school... at least the first thirty-five pages!" Laughter. They cited the class, the teacher, some class anecdotes.

They talked about the rock concerts Mike went to. Where did he get all those concert tickets? Laughter.

They told the story about Mike and the librarian. She would take away Mike's suckers, holding out her hand. "Just one more lick," he'd say. And then he'd put the wet end in her hand. THE WET END! The whole table convulsed in laughter.

Son John came in from playing hockey and joined the discussion.

They talked about a fight. Mike wasn't scared. Not in school, not in soccer. Not in the family. Not in life. He was strong.

And dancing. "He danced?" asked Dan, amazed. "Remember, John, we could never get him to dance at home."

But the kids swore he was a good dancer. They told the story that once Michael paid off the DJ at a bar mitzvah to have him play Stevie Wonder's "I Just Called to Say I Love You." Nobody else would have had the nerve to do that. He had the nerve!

The students and family were now loose, the memories flowing like water, with laughter as well as sadness. Dan and David and John reveled in the feast of details. Through it all, Mike's cat sat on the table.

Finally the students said they had to get back to school. But it was clear that this morning spent with the Shulman family was part of a lesson they would never forget. "Thank you, Mr. Shulman," they said at the door.

"Thank *you*," said Dan. "It's such fun to hear about Mike."

Then Dan showed me a poem he had written. He and Margaret and David and Amy were traveling when Michael died, and he scrawled it on the back of a folded-up crossword puzzle during the long plane ride home.

> *It rained the morning I came home after*
> *your death. I wrote these words in tears, my boy,*
> *my beautiful boy, I lost my boy,*
> *Mike. This is my torn and racked heart.*
> *I cannot make it rhyme or fit, like my grief.*
> *When I see people I say, "I lost my boy."*
> *I have to say it, hear it, force it from*
> *myself. O darling boy, forever lost.*
> *I close my eyes. I kiss your sleeping eyes.*
> *Your empty room. Your awful absence.*
> *This poem is like my life. I have no more words.*
> *And yet I need to go on, syllable by*
> *syllable, day by day, to the task I have*
> *set myself, my beautiful, beautiful boy.*

Ultimately, the Shulman family did not just learn a lesson in grief. It gave one.

Like Dan and Margaret Shulman and their family, the community goes about the tasks it has set for itself, syllable by syllable, day by day. Wounded. Less certain now about justice and order in the universe. But full again of daily dreams and details. And hopeful, too, that the mysterious slayers of children are rendered at least marginally less powerful by our shared grief.

A Horrible Cat Story

(February 1988)

I have a horrible story to tell.

Fifteen years ago a cat came into our family's life. Our eldest daughter—a child then, a wiser woman now—innocently put out a small pan of milk on our back porch for a little furry stray.

Since then, the soft, purry, rubby, affectionate little thing has brought the Coyote family fifteen years of uninterrupted . . . allergies, cat hair, footprints on the car, meowing for food, purring on our faces at three in the morning, ferocious kitty litter smells, kitty litter spilled, cat food spilled, and fights in the family about whose responsibility it is to feed the cat, change the litter, and clean up after all of it.

Not to the mention catfights at night. And male cat spray all around the yard. And the vet's neutering bill. And cat urine around the house.

And the old stuck-on-the-second-story-ledge-in-the-dead-of-night trick, which included scratching on the second story window until someone got up and let him in. We hated him for that.

Blood turned against blood. The Littlest Coyote, now seven years old, who has known the cat all her life, considers her familiarity a license for abuse. She stuffs him into boxes. Wraps him up in baby clothes and bonnets. Ties ropes from neck to paw and back to neck so if he moves he chokes.

We as parents—flinty-hearted and catnasty as we are—cannot bear this mistreatment, and urge our daughter to behave, yell at our own flesh-and-blood daughter to leave the fur-and-blood feline alone, release it from that shoebox this instant, on and on, without noticeable effect except one more family hassle.

And the shredded upholstery. We bought scratching posts, but the cat loved the couch fabric more. So we bought anti-cat sprays. The cat loved the anti-cat sprays. So we bought squirt guns. They worked great, but of course someone had to be around to squirt the cat in the eye at precisely the moment he began shredding, which someone rarely was (but I have to admit squirting the cat was very satisfying). Finally the squirt guns were expropriated by one child or another for higher purposes, like shooting each other, and then the guns disappeared, and that was that.

And the cat was the cat. Sleeping. Eating. Ageless. Walking on our faces or scratching and crying outside in the night.

Which brings us to the unexpected present we received this Christmas season.

Saturday two weeks before Christmas was the kind of day we have too few of these greenhouse seasons, the cold so sharp it takes your breath away.

While our family was out running errands, our new neighbor heard the cat scratching at our back door—which he has done successfully for fifteen years. A cat fancier herself, she thought the furry little thing was going to freeze to death, so she catnapped him and put him into her heated garage, then went about her business. She knew that several people went in and out of the garage every day and that the cat could easily get out after he had a chance to warm up.

The neighbor later alerted Mrs. Coyote about her action, and went over with her to the garage. Mrs. C called the cat's name—that's a joke, what cat knows its name?—but the cat never responded. They both assumed that the cat had freaked out at such unprecedented care and had run off. He would come back. He always has.

But he didn't come back. Not for three weeks.

My wife dutifully searched the local pounds. She put up posters. She even took the grieving little one to the animal shelter and pawed over new kittens. All for show, mind you, because in the back of her mind, Mrs. Coyote felt a growing spark of hope. FINALLY, WE ARE RID OF HIM!!!

New Year's Day. After a rare night of extended celebration and therefore getting to bed very late, we were dead asleep at seven in the morning when the phone rang. It was the neighbor. She could hear the cat meowing. In her garage.

Mrs. Coyote stumbled out into the frozen air in her bathrobe. The neighbor met her in the garage. No sign of the cat. And no noise. My wife was now positive the neighbor was crazy.

Just as she was about to stumble back to bed, she heard a faint meow. Digging behind some ancient storm windows, she found him.

She called me on the phone. Guess where I was. ZZZZZ. I stumbled out to the garage. I dragged away the ancient storm windows. There was the cat, filthy and forlorn, deep under a stairway where he could easily have exited on his own if he had wanted. I picked him up. He weighed practically nothing. His yellow eyes were sunk deep into his head.

We carried him home. We offered him food and milk. He tasted only a bit, then ran frenzied throughout the house as if he recognized nothing. The slightest noise startled him. Occasionally he wobbled. Then he hid under our bed, refusing to come out.

My wife and the Littlest One spent most of New Year's Day at the vet emergency room. Dr. Vet felt him. "Your cat is virtually dead," he said. "Kidney failure. Organs atrophied. Only a slight chance of survival, if we put him on an IV overnight. Cost you $110. Probably hopeless. I recommend you say good-bye."

Our chance! An honorable end to this fifteen-year scourge. Pay $110 for a cat that clearly wants to die? Get serious.

We paid the $110. OK, said the vet, but say your good-byes anyway.

One last question, Doctor, Mrs. C. asked. Why did the cat stay in that garage for three weeks, with nary a cry nor an escape to our house one door away until New Year's Day at 7 a.m.? No idea, said the vet.

The next day, the phone rang. I answered. It was Dr. Vet. Give me the bad news, Doctor, I said. Actually, he said, your cat has made a remarkable recovery. You can pick him up anytime.

The receiver dropped from my hand.

Last evening, I sat on the shredded living room couch alternately reading a book and watching our daughter dance to music from the stereo. She was dancing with the cat, holding him upside down. She brought the cat to me and put him in my lap while she continued to dance. So much for reading. I found myself cheering my daughter's graceful twirling. My hands, of their own accord, entwined in the long soft fur of the vibrating cat on my lap. The feeling was warm. My hands stroked, and stroked, and stroked.

Dukakis or Not to Caucus: That's No Question

(February 1988)

The last Tuesday of February is the time Minnesotans attend precinct caucuses. This year participants will select their party's nominee for President of the United States. Everyone of voting age should attend, but few will.

As a Presidential selection mechanism, precinct caucuses are impractical. A primary election samples the pulse of the general public much more accurately. In addition, far more voters participate when a whole evening isn't required. Voting is familiar, understandable, anonymous.

All of which makes precinct caucuses a silly way to nominate a candidate for President who must gain favor with the average voter in November.

Still, the caucus system holds a huge, unheralded benefit: Caucuses provide valuable access into the serious life of the community. Attendance is wide-open, no political pedigrees or party references required. One need only the desire to work for a party, a candidate or a cause. If one can make that leap of commitment, one will always have a community wherever one lives.

At least that's how precinct caucuses worked for me.

When we moved to Minnesota temporarily in 1972, we didn't know what a political precinct was, not to mention a caucus. We also didn't know anyone who lived in the area except an obstetrician.

We had come from nearby western Wisconsin, my wife pregnant with our third child. Our Twin Cities obstetrician pioneered natural childbirth in which the father participates in the birth process, revolutionary back then. We broke off a trip to return to the area to have our baby with him.

We located an apartment through the University of Minnesota housing services. We moved at the beginning of December, my wife big as a water buffalo. We planned to stay through the March birth, then move on to my new teaching job in Massachusetts that summer. We knew nothing about the neighborhood.

Six months later we didn't want to leave. Why?

Strongly opposed to the Viet Nam war, I became involved in George McGovern's campaign for the Democratic nomination for President. That led us to attend many pre-caucus organizational meetings in neighborhood living rooms. Then we knocked on doors throughout the area handing out pamphlets and discussing issues. We took busses to outlying towns to canvass voters. We urged everyone to attend his or her precinct caucus. Finally, on the last Tuesday in February, we attended our own precinct caucus, our first ever. We found it jam-packed with new neighborhood friends.

What happened politically after that is public knowledge. My candidate lost the election big. Richard Nixon later broke into the offices of his opponents and opened up China. Both made lasting contributions to American political life.

For ordinary citizens, participation in the precinct caucus system offers a lasting contribution to community life.

You meet extraordinary people committed enough to take an active part in the political life of their neighborhood, their city, their state and their country, willing to give up a Tuesday night for a cause larger than themselves.

All their time and effort is unpaid and possibly unrewarded with political victory, but contains rich payments and victories nonetheless.

When we decided to move back to Minnesota from Massachusetts two years later, I mistakenly worried with Thomas Wolfian somberness that "you can't go home again." I had forgotten how many people we had met here in our brief political effort. When we returned, they welcomed us back. We learned that precinct is another word for neighborhood.

So attend your precinct caucus on Tuesday. It may be an inefficient way to nominate candidates for President, but it's a brilliant means of finding your way home.

The Urban Coyote Is "On Vacation"

(April 1988)

This Florida vacation would be different. This year I wouldn't spend most of the week working at a desk in our rented room, listening to the kids enjoy the beautiful sunshine. Even if the neighborhood newspaper had to get by with that stock phrase *"The columnist is on vacation,"* I'd hit the beach for sure.

The problem began when I was packing. I noticed that I was putting four pounds of student term papers into my bag, along with three special red pens with which to inscribe pithy comments about the work. Grades were due the week I returned.

Next to them were the background files for the three ads

that I was supposed to have finished for the company before I left. I'd do them on the beach between correcting papers.

Next to them were five books, all long-standing members of the Urban Coyote Must Read List which has grown longer and longer the last twenty-five years, in spite of my recent participation in a reading group. No wonder I am out of it when I talk to people. "Have you read the latest biography of the President?" they ask. "Which President?" I answer. "I'm still working on Grover Cleveland." As for novels, someone reminded me recently that I seem to have missed entire continents of literature and I'd better get with it. "What do you know of traditional Vietnamese literature?" he asked. "You mean that you are ignorant of French Dadaist fiction?" another inquired. "Here, read this," Mrs. Coyote said, shoving a sixth book into my bag, *The Awakening* by Kate Chopin. I glanced at the dust jacket. "This pioneering turn-of-the-century short novel of feminist fiction is a sympathetic portrayal of a woman's discovery of the stifling bonds of her marriage and the strengthening of her sexuality." Oh great. I haven't read Anäis Nin yet either.

What else to bring? Nothing more from the office. They'll Federal Express the annual report to me for editing once I arrive. I'll do it on the beach.

Why then am I bringing my computer? Hey, that's fun, not work. I get to catch up on writing projects in my hotel room, then transmit back to my office via modem. Miracle of electronics. I can bring my office right with me. I'm so excited. When the other family members clear out to hit the beach and catch some solar rays, I get to hit the keys and bask in cathode rays. Maybe I'll write my Urban Coyote column after all.

Don't get me wrong, I did hit the beach, the first day.

It was warm, sunny, perfectly clear, exactly what you don't want on the first day in Florida if you are coming from Minnesota. Somehow my family mixed up #20 sun grease with #2 sun grease, using them both. The next day we were all streaked, parts of our bodies suffering second-degree burns, red as solar flares, other parts as white as Minnesota snow. The whole family looked like psychedelic zebras. Bad trip.

The next day the wind cooled the air, but the sun was bright and clear, a fatal combination for the innocent. My wife and kids overcooked themselves totally this time, to the point that they were not amused. Nor was I. Since I was not in pain, I became their slave.

Why wasn't I sunburned along with them? Because I was at the airport. Son #2 was to arrive from college, an easy two-hour pickup. But he missed his plane because he spent too much time searching for the tennis racquet he had loaned to a friend six months before—no big problem since he ended up forgetting his tennis shoes anyway—but I waited until sunset for his next plane. Waiting for him, I had the opportunity to hang out indoors at the airport all day while the sun raked hallucinogenic heat waves over the surrounding acres of black asphalt. No burn for me.

I actually read an entire novel in the airport lounge. Not any of the novels I brought with me, of course, but one given to me at the last minute by a Florida friend who insisted that it was a "must read, you'll love it, let's talk about it." It wasn't, I didn't, he left.

The next day I began to drink. What is it about rum and vacation? I rarely drink at home. I can't finish an entire beer these days without falling asleep, and I never drink liquor. One of the benefits of over forty years of life experience has been the discovery that booze acts as a soporific for me. I used to be famous for falling asleep at parties, my face in the soup.

Yet here I was next to a pool within sight of beaches and ocean and palm trees and suddenly I found my hand curled around a sequence of fruit concoctions laced with dark rum. I tried to read but fell sound asleep before noon, student papers fluttering in the wind around me, a novel spread open and unread on my chest leaving a permanent unsunburned imprint like a white flag of surrender.

So I over-ate. What is it about vacations and food? I never eat breakfast at home, and all my lunches are lightweight. Here it's three meals *uber alles*. I feel as if I've swallowed a blowfish.

So I decided to get a little exercise. I went for a run. But I had packed economically for a change, and I did not bring my running shoes, so ran in my tennis shoes, giving me shin splints for two days.

Which was OK, because a cold front came through. Since I had packed economically, I brought nothing warm. I was suddenly freezing to death. Worse than Minnesota. I spent a whole day searching tacky shopping malls looking for a sweatshirt that didn't say "Life is a beach" across the chest.

I was torn between one that somewhat subtly promoted a prominent French windsurfer brand and one with a huge illustration of a fishing boat holding a fisherman reaching for dark rectangular objects floating in the water. The inscription read: "Save the bales." To think these guys actually used to catch fish down here.

The next day dawned with a clear sky plus plenty of wind for windsurfing and riding the waves. I could barely contain my excitement as I finished working at my computer before noon and headed for the beach. The Atlantic rollers streamed in as far as the eye could see under flags standing straight toward shore. What is that sign? DANGER—SEA PESTS! I walked along the margin of the waves. All along the beach were fresh carcasses of Portuguese men-of-war, savage reminders of the hell that awaited anyone who ventured one foot into the surf. Their lavender balloons sailed the wave crests and bobbed in the seafoam. Damn, we don't have those things in northern lakes.

I got some exercise, anyway. I chased student papers all over the beach in the strong wind.

By the last day, my vacation rhythm was well established. I'd get up early, before the rest of the family moved their exhausted, tanned muscles. I'd drink a pot of coffee and read the paper. Just like home. Then after they got up and hit the beach, I'd move into the bedroom, set up the computer, and type. My only remaining deadline was this "on vacation" column to transmit to the icy urban neighborhoods of the North. Then I'd hit the beach too. Great. Because this morning the sun shone like warm white gold and the sky was as clear as my computer screen.

As I typed these final lines, my wife returned from the beach, dusting sand from her shoulders. "I'm finishing my vacation column," I told her. "Great," she answered. "I'm coming inside. Big black clouds are rolling in—rain clouds."

Great, I said. Coyote is on vacation. Life is a beach.

The Drought of '88

(September 1988)

My family spent our summer vacation on an island in the Great Lakes.

We didn't have a television or a radio or newspapers. The short term disasters that normally occupy us—exploding gas mains, fateful exchanges of missiles in the Mideast, wars of words among politicians, rapes and murders and lawsuits and legislative wrangling and business successes and failures—we let them all disappear for a week.

But the biggest story of the season wouldn't go away.

Every day the sun rose fiery hot in a sky without even a wisp of cirrus cloud.

We Midwesterners are used to considering the sun a friendly force. We treasure our short, clear winter days and celebrate the sun's long climb to the summer sky. But not this year. This year the sun became our enemy in early spring, and grew even more ferocious as spring turned into summer.

This year the sun was implacable—a word calling up images from old French Foreign Legion films set in North African deserts with heroes in torn uniforms and minds driven mad by thirst.

Every day the sun beat down, not bringing life but death—first for the flowers, then the grass, then the young boulevard trees, then the farmers' crops.

And the wind was the hostile sun's ally. It brought no relief, but only more heat, more like a blacksmith's bellows than a summer breeze.

Normally the deep, cold waters of the Great Lakes inspire confidence. Not this year. I watched mists rise up off the lake under the unrelenting eye of the sun, millions of gallons of fresh water evaporating in front of me. I felt the water get so warm that we could swim around in it at a leisurely pace instead of the frantic, chilled bursts normal at that time of year. And I felt fear.

Fear for the farmers, fear for the food supply and the wildlife, fear for the trees and fresh water that surrounded us in such abundance, and fear that our atmosphere has finally become so corrupted that the trend may be irreversible.

My fear was not entirely rational, I know. My rational mind is a student of geologic time. I know that the history of these lakes includes long cycles of rising and falling. My own memory reminds me that the Great Lakes reached record *high* levels due to excessive rainfall only three years ago.

But I am also a student of history and ecology. As our civilization burns more and more fossil fuel, even a system as vast and complex as the atmosphere could be affected. The transparent, life-giving atmospheric blanket, now filling with fossil fuel waste, may be contributing to the heating and shriveling of life around us. The chickens of our energy-intensive economy may be coming home to roost.

No rain has fallen on the island for over two months. The normally cool nights are hot and sticky. The yellow hawkweed bloomed weeks early. A horse chestnut tree on the main street already dropped its seeds. Instead of the familiar meaty chestnuts, they are the size of dried peas.

The irony is that these are ideal vacation days. Not a cloud in the sky. Kids play outside, swimming, riding bikes, walking among the innumerable yellow wildflowers that survive in the cool shadows of the cedar forest.

Yet every day I scanned the skies and worried. Could we have botched the planet?

As we packed our suitcases to return home, tongues of gray cumulus clouds slowly appeared over the back of the island. As we took the ferry to the mainland, clouds covered the sun and shaded us for the first time in two weeks. We found our car covered with sticky dust.

As we drove west toward home, the clouds turned black and hung like ragged skirts over the treetops. Then a few sprinkles dotted the windshield, just as we drove through a section of forest blackened into a series of giant medieval spikes by a recent fire.

And then the downpour began. The rain fell stronger and stronger as we drove. We felt our car getting clean for the first time all year. We could hear the wildflowers and the birds and the farmers singing in the fields.

As we continued westward, the sun returned, first in sprays of light through the clouds, then etching the boiling cumulus in mauve and gold. We realized that it is the presence of clouds, and the moisture within them, that makes a sunset truly beautiful.

We are home now. The neighborhood remains parched, the lawns and trees brown and lifeless. But school will soon start. The newspaper will thump on the doorstep with news of missiles and business. The deadlines of work will begin again. The days, still hot, will cool.

But I do not want to forget that fear. Whatever the cause of the heat and drought of the summer of 1988, I do not believe cool September weather is the end of it.

Center of the Neighborhood

(October 1988)

Early in our tenure in the neighborhood, some families began to agitate with the park board and city council for a recreation center, a facility most city neighborhoods had. Neighborhood opponents argued that we didn't need such an eyesore—that kids should play outside in the park, not inside in a stuffy building, and no one was having kids anymore anyway. As a coach of several burgeoning youth basketball teams, frustrated by a lack of practice space, I weighed in on the side of the center. We won, and the Kenwood Park Center was built as part of a renovated Kenwood School, the first such collaboration between the Park Board and School Board in the city.

I recently drove down to the Kenwood Park Center with my teenage son to evaluate that neighborhood decision in some detail.

We picked up a basketball game with Paul Jaeger, a long-time gym rat who lives a block away from the Center. He is now six feet tall and employed part-time to run the desk. We played free-form twenty-one.

I opened hot, sinking several spectacular jump shots over the outstretched hands of my frenzied opponents. I followed by swishing my first two free throws.

How was it, then, that I quickly fell behind? Unfortunately, I ran into a series of unsuspected hazards.

Hazard #1. Unbeknownst to me, my son, just turned sixteen, had developed a double-pump lay-up. Must have been practicing at school. Also, he showed amazing vigor on the boards, garnering approximately eighty percent of the early rebounds through sheer hustle. I don't recall that much hustle at the kitchen sink or with the lawn mower. Turns out the kid can move after all.

Hazard #2. The Park Center Rat had the last word. He maintained a twinkle in his eye, not to mention a witty repartee, throughout the game, as if he were keeping a secret from the old guy. The secret turned out to be that he had the best outside shot. Final score: 21 Rat, 19 Teenaged Coyote, 16 Urban Coyote.

But I survived. Given multiple additional hazards, this was an ego-building accomplishment.

Hazard #3. The gymnasium floor. It had been waxed recently with a substance that gave the linoleum the slipperiness of fresh ice. The Rat said the Park Board bought inferior wax. Good thing I'm not an attorney or I'd send potential clients to the gym for instant groin pulls and huge lawsuits.

Hazard #4. My body. The slick floor, plus basketball's challenge to infrequently exploited tendons and muscle groups, caused pains to appear all over my body. Only one or two of them persist several days later as I write this, I am pleased to report.

Hazard #5. Six-year-old Nathaniel Feldman. He is an up-and-coming Park Center Rat. He hangs out there on a regular basis and I believe aspires to Paul Jaeger's exalted position in twelve years or so. He was shooting hoops with a grapefruit-sized ball at the other end of the court, but his exuberance simply could not be contained by only half the court. His red ball frequently bounded into our game, with him thundering right after it. Amazing we didn't break our ankles stepping on the ball or Nathaniel's head.

Hazard #6. The Youngest Coyote. Also six years old, she

quietly played floor hockey in another corner of the gym. Normally a shy one, she tends to play "within herself," as the sports commentators put it. Not this time. Slap shots skidded the length of the floor through our unwary feet. She smiled at us with the kind of triumph that Olympic victory usually brings.

Hazard #7. The smell of popcorn emanating from the common room. I found it very hard to concentrate on basketball with such scents in the air. I found it even harder to play basketball with one hand covered with popcorn grease.

Hazard #8. Aerobics class in the activity room. This hazard was purely psychological, as the activity room door was closed and the thumping workout music could barely be heard in the gym and certainly I couldn't see the writhing, mostly female bodies. Nevertheless, I had reason to believe that Mrs. Coyote was in there. So was Sheila the Great Aerobics Instructor. And half the pulchritude and three-quarters of the IQ of the entire neighborhood. All paying a buck fifty per class to tune up their portfolios. Even as I sweated in serious, head-to-head male-bonding basketball with the Teenaged Coyote and the Rat, a certain part of my mind couldn't help wandering toward aerobics class. I felt the need to visit the aerobics room. Look in the door. Say hello. Ask a question. Uhh, excuse me—beat, da, da, beat, beat, da, da—what is the capital of Soviet Georgia? Anybody know? Do wop do wop. OK, thanks.

The park center closed at six-thirty.

Mrs. Coyote, Sheila the Great and various other neighborhood Intellectuals strode perspiring out of the aerobics class while I stood, perspiring, waiting. Mrs. C. chased down the Little One, who had run to the outdoor play area. They walked home together.

I rode home in the car, giving the teenager some badly needed driving practice, as he had recently obtained his learner's permit. I am pleased to report that he has all the makings of a safe, responsible driver, albeit not soon.

I remember when the neighborhood had no park center. No place where teaching is done with slick jump shots and double-pump lay-ups among fathers and sons and neighborhood kids that have watched each other grow up. No place where bodies can be sharpened so that minds may be cleared. No place where community is centered and maintained.

I remember the political fight to gain such a facility for our neighborhood. It was well worth winning.

The Battle of the Curbs

(November 1988)

This is the story of a victory of light over darkness. Of hope over despair. Of the individual over bureaucracy. Of neighborhood over city. Of air over asphalt.

It includes a bare-knuckled conflict between the industrial powers of The Machine and the ancient weapons of a woman who waters her flowers.

It is the Battle of the Curbs, and I am pleased to be its Homer.

This year our neighborhood transportation grid transformed into a litter box of torn up streets and torn out curbs. The city paving contractors were hard at dusty work replacing the existing curbs and gutters—installed at the time of the Pharaohs—with fresh new ones. In the process, they were replacing street surfaces, sewer connections, storm drains, catch basins, gas lines and whatever else they inadvertently dug up with their backhoes.

In spite of the resulting cloud of dust, the shaking of our house foundation by tamping machines, the distinct sewer gas smell that lasted for weeks and the rust that flowed from our faucets, in spite of having no place to park our cars and a moat of mud around the house after every rain, in spite of all this for six months, we were overjoyed to know that new curbs were coming.

Our old curbs were despicable. Is that too strong? No, we despised them.

One does not realize how much one cares about curbs until they crumble away. Ours had crumbled years ago, like concrete icebergs calving from glaciers to litter the street.

The front of our house was an obstacle course of dislodged curb chunks. Our family's already grumpy push lawn mower chipped its teeth on the chunks that remained in place. The grumpy teenagers pushing the grumpy lawn mower refused to negotiate the bumpy terrain and left clumps of grass behind to grow tall, yellow and die.

So we cared about curbs.

For five years we waited for curb repair. The city promised that this would be the year. We waited all summer while the streets around our block were gutted, re-curbed, cleaned and gleaming. We waited. The dust in the neighborhood coated everything, including Mrs. Coyote's beloved garden. We waited. Only with the first colors of fall did the curb crew finally turn toward our intersection.

The city's crews ripped out the old curbs plus the street.

Then they cut away a foot or two of parkway lawn. Then they graded the edges, installed a guide wire, and prepared for the coming of The Machine.

Let me tell you about The Machine.

It looks like a monster spider on tracks. Prior to the invention of The Machine, workers had to place forms, pour concrete, let it dry, then strip the forms. Now The Machine does all that with one automated pass down an entire block following the guide wire. Only at corners do traditional concrete forms still need to be used.

The Machine is an invention of an Iowa farmer who reportedly combined his knowledge of manure slurries with that of conveyor belts. He is now building himself a huge stone castle in the heart of an Iowa cornfield. According to the local workers, The Machine cost eight hundred jobs in the Twin Cities, a perfect example of progress. One clever guy gets himself a castle; eight hundred guys look for new jobs.

Mrs. Coyote, in her daily attention to her dusty, depressed garden, took to monitoring construction progress. She chatted with the construction workers and admired the various yawning caverns they dug and then filled and then dug again around our house.

One day she noticed that more of our parkway lawn had been removed than elsewhere in the neighborhood.

Was the city widening our street, she wondered? Couldn't be, said I. Curb guys are honorable men and nothing in the plan mentions street widening.

She called Alderman Carlson's office for an explanation. Carlson's assistant, Ms. Julie, called right back.

She said she hadn't spoken directly with Mr. L., the engineer in charge of this paving project, but one of Mr. L's assistants showed her the blueprints and yes indeed, you are right, they are widening your street. By a foot. City policy is to make all streets thirty-two feet wide, and your block is only thirty-one feet. They measured from center of the street and decided to take the full foot off your side. Mrs. C. growled.

Ms. Julie and Mr. L. agreed to stop further work on our street until this matter could be aired. End of Day One.

The next day Mrs. Coyote was again watering her dusty garden and chatting with the street workers. They couldn't believe it. Somebody had complained about one lousy foot and stopped the project. They were incredulous.

Take a look around, said Mrs. Coyote. Note that this block has only five houses on it. Do you see anybody else outside? They did not. Then I'm the one who stopped the project. They turned purple with embarrassment.

Ms. Julie was able to set up a conference call between Mr. L., herself, and Mrs. C.

The policy, he reiterated, is to make all city streets uniform at thirty-two feet. We measured from the center of the street and determined that the foot should come entirely off your side. To make any changes at this time will be costly. The catch basins have been sited and will have to be moved. But we can compromise. We'll give you six inches.

If you can give me back six inches, you can give me a foot, said Mrs. C.

She remembered that the nearby Franklin Avenue repaving project required public hearings before the street could be widened. The city can't widen streets without a public hearing, she announced desperately.

That's right, confirmed Ms. Julie.

Mrs. C. warmed to the topic. Every blade of grass in the city is important, she said. Asphalt is hot and noisy. Grass gives us oxygen to breathe. This is not just one foot. This is one foot times the length of the block, or over three hundred square feet of life-giving oxygen!

There was a brief silence over the phone followed by a sigh of resignation. OK, said Mr. L, we'll give you back your foot.

OK, said Mrs. C. And we do not expect to be assessed for the additional costs incurred. This is your problem, not ours.

And one final thing, piped up Mrs. C. I am one of the few women in the neighborhood still "in the home," as they say, so I'll be checking on you.

End of Day Two.

Two days later, The Machine was again fired up and rumbling toward us. Mrs. C. was out watering her dusty, depressed garden and chatting with the street guys, now friends.

Wait a minute, you can't turn that corner, she commanded, pointing down the street. You forgot to remeasure and move the guide stakes!

Her Guys looked at her. They had reassembled the corner forms with much labor. The Machine was rumbling up behind them toward the turn.

Mrs. C. looked at them. They looked at her. Then she made it easy for them. I am going to lie down in front of The Machine if it tries to turn this corner.

The supervisor looked up. You got a coffeepot? he asked.

Mrs. C. ran into the house and brewed a fresh pot. She brought out a fresh loaf of homemade bread as well.

The coffee break was on. The Machine ground to a halt.

Two days later, all stakes had been properly remeasured and replaced. The Machine was again on its way.

Mrs. C. was again out watering the dusty, depressed flowers and chatting with Her Guys. Something still didn't look right. She glared at the supervisor.

The city immediately dispatched another engineer to the house to go over the re-measurements with Mrs. C. Well, she said, I guess that's better.

The Machine rumbled around the corner and up the block, curbing as it went.

Of all the members of the city's curb crew, only one remained skeptical of the costly remediation they had undertaken the past week. He still couldn't believe the fight over one stupid foot.

But the other guys seemed actually to have enjoyed this triumphant howl of the grass roots. They could taste the fresh air. They could smell the coffee.

The Sounds of Silence

(May 1989)

I bought a new car. Not only was my old one was coughing to death, but I liked the stereo in the new one. No, scratch that, I loved the stereo. It is a fundamental truth of American males that they cannot resist foxy stereos.

My attraction to high tech electronics is otherwise inexplicable, since I rarely listen to the car radio. When I do, it is exclusively public radio news and information, the kind of fare that does not require graphic equalizers, auto-reverse tape decks, four speakers and forty watts per channel.

In fact, I have a strong antipathy for the welter of electronic noise and gizmos in the general environment—AM, FM, MTV, CNN, ESPN, records, tapes, CDs, all are cultural pollution, that's what I say.

Furthermore, I believe the Sony Walkman to be the most soul-destroying invention since the boombox, stealing a person's last chance to escape into the quiet recesses of one's own skull. If one can never listen for one's own internal music, how can one ever hope to find it?

All that said, I fell hard for this foxy stereo with a four-door car attached.

The dials were all illuminated. The station preset buttons were big enough to actually see while driving. It had a built-in graphic equalizer, something that was new and hot in 1984 and therefore very desirable, even though I had little idea what it was, no idea how to use it and no use for it anyway.

The car worked fine. The radio, however, had problems.

Within a week, it couldn't hold a radio signal. Within two weeks, it was dead.

I returned to the dealership. Yes, they said, there have been many problems with those radios. You can replace it with the same model, but it probably won't work either. Or you can replace it with a factory-approved alternate, a better radio with Dolby® noise reduction, albeit without the sexy graphic equalizer and with fiendishly small station preset buttons.

I didn't want to risk additional radio disappointment. I took the substitute.

The next day, one of the front speakers developed an annoying rattle, as if mosquitoes were operating tiny chain saws inside.

I went back to the dealer. The speaker was replaced.

The buzz continued. Another trip to the dealer and another speaker was replaced. Buzz, rattle, hiss.

Back again. This time all four speakers were replaced. As I drove out of the service garage I turned on the radio. The mosquitoes started their chain saws the moment the sun hit the car.

The service manager had never heard of anything like this. He subtly suggested that I scrap the whole damn stereo system. After additional months of speaker rattle madness and sparring with nonexistent factory zone managers, I concluded that he was right.

I scrapped the old system for a brand new Alpine stereo with four brand new Alpine speakers. Finally the sound was as crisp and clean as it was on the first test drive of the car two years before. More important, the system again looked good. The dashboard was bathed in sexy green stereo luminescence.

I parked the car in my driveway on a gentle Sunday afternoon a few days later. Just after sunset, a friend of my son's surprised an itinerant gentleman lying on the floor of my car prying at the speakers. The gentleman retreated in haste. The speakers survived. The radio was stolen.

With the insurance money, minus the deductible, I ordered a new radio, this time the removable kind. It cost $50 more, but this radio wouldn't be stolen. No way. I would carry it inside the house every night.

A few days later I arrived home from work, the mellifluous news analysis of NPR's Cokie Roberts and Nina Totenberg ringing joyfully in my ears. I parked the car in the driveway. Halfway out, I stopped. Ah ha! I had forgotten to remove the removable radio. I leaned back in to do so.

Here I must pause to describe three details, two of them

geographic. First, the radio was positioned right in front of the shift lever so that I had to ease the car out of "park" and pull back the shift lever to get the radio all the way out. Second, my emergency brake had never worked properly in spite of having it repaired at great expense a week earlier. Third, my driveway slopes toward the street, with concrete walls on both sides that narrow toward the street entrance.

Back to the action. With my left foot still out the door, I pulled hard on the emergency brake (just "fixed"), then took the car out of "park" and pulled the radio part way out. Then I noticed the car was rolling backward.

Oh oh.

I jammed the shift lever back into "park," but it wouldn't go in. I jammed my right foot onto the floor brake, but missed. I couldn't close the driver's side door because my left leg was hanging out.

At which point the door caught on the concrete wall and peeled backward like a butterfly wing. Two thousand dollars damage, plus a huge increase in insurance rates due to this expensive "moving" accident. Two miles an hour in my driveway! I screamed at the insurance agent on the phone. He merely sighed.

Two weeks later I picked up the car with the shiny new door and parked in my office parking lot right across the street from J. D. Hoyt's restaurant. I always feel comfortable parking there because at least two police cars are always parked on the street—the police love to eat at Hoyt's—so I left the radio behind. I returned at five o'clock. That's odd. Someone has accidentally thrown a stone through my rear passenger window. How else could it have been broken? Then I noticed that my driver's side door was unlocked.

Oh oh.

The removable radio was removed, this time with the housing from which it was removable. Broad daylight, in front of two police cars. Nothing left but speakers.

I am a slow learner, but I finally got the message. No car radio. Since then, I have substituted the musings of silence for those of "Morning Edition" and "All Things Considered." Where the radio once lived now sits a small packet of Kleenex and a notebook on which I write.

Silence. It has changed my life.

In the silence of early morning drive time, I have rediscovered freedom and creativity. In the early morning silence, I have rediscovered enthusiasm. In the early morning silence, I have made connections among the welter of information already in my head. In the early morning drive time silence, I wrote a book.

But I am still an American male. Is it possible to have a full life with a Kleenex packet instead of a radio? Also, at the end of the work day I am hardly creative. My head has turned into a grapefruit, feeling soft, squishy and slightly bitter. So this year I secretly bought a Walkman-type radio, which I kept in my glove compartment and furtively stuck into my ears on the way home for an "All Things" fix, until my son reprimanded me sternly, saying that what I was doing was illegal driving behavior.

OK. OK. I still had the old car radio—the one that created all the speaker static—in a dusty grocery bag in the basement. Just last week I dug it out and ordered it installed during the car's spring tune-up. For afternoon use only, I told myself. Surely the static problem would disappear with my surviving Alpine speakers.

The next day the service advisor called. "Where did you get that radio, at a garage sale?" It wouldn't work at all. And he had already invested an hour and a half installing it (at $49.50 an hour).

Do you hear what I hear? Clearly I am intended to drive in silence, to listen to my own stories.

As I drive I again take up my notebook. Holding the steering wheel with one hand, I write down the stories that come to me. A very dangerous turn in life. But not as dangerous as a radio.

Deer Tales

(June 1989)

According to local Park Center Rat Paul Jaeger, the sign and spoor and scat of deer have been around our urban neighborhood all winter. Cross-country skiers have reported quantities of two-toed deer tracks around the island in Lake of the Isles. Paul's brother saw a doe with two fawns on the north side of Cedar Lake, next to the railroad tracks near downtown.

But nothing prepared Paul for last December. Here's the story he told.

About 9 p.m., Paul left his house right behind Kenwood School. As he drove past the intersection between the school and Kenwood Park, a deer leaped in front of his car.

He slammed on his brakes, thinking that the vaulting shadow was some crazed teenaged skateboarder. Instead, a magnificent ten-point buck stood in the intersection in a pool of streetlight. It had to weigh two hundred pounds, Paul whistled to himself.

This was a particular shock to Paul, an ardent bow hunter. "We go bow hunting once a week in the longbow season. We sit in the trees. We freeze. We don't see a thing. Then the biggest buck I have ever seen turns up in Kenwood Park a half block from my house!"

He stopped his car. The buck was fifteen to twenty feet away. They looked at each other a long time. Finally the buck gracefully bounded away toward Kenwood Parkway and was gone.

Paul agrees that the story is incredible, but he's sticking with it. But you know young people. Prone to hallucinations at any moment. Too much TV. Too much late night coffee. Too much beer mixed with chips and salsa.

Still, he does have credibility. He definitely knows the difference between a deer and a dog. Last bow season he bagged a buck in the Minnesota River valley on the urban fringe. He has perfected legal urban deer-hunting techniques. "You put on running gear, they think you're a jogger," he smiles.

Would a man with this much sophistication enter a false urban deer report? Still, the sighting is impossible.

Ours is, after all, a major metropolitan area, home to multiple Fortune 500 corporations, major league orchestras, theaters, art museums, public radio and television stations, sports teams, Prince and the 1992 Super Bowl, not to mention the basketball Timberwolves, the mortal enemy of deer.

And ours is, after all, an urban neighborhood, situated cheek-by-fang between the financial canyons of downtown Minneapolis and the sophisticated Soho of Uptown, immediate home of Sebastian Joe's ice cream and coffee parlor, dry cleaners, bike shops, religious institutions and taxes so high as to become religious statements in themselves.

Can we also be home to wildness as well? No way.

Wildness means few people, low taxes and black flies. Wildness means bumpy back roads and wood ticks and wood smoke. Wildness means your paddle floats away and is consumed by beavers, not your bicycle is stolen and trucked to Chicago.

Minneapolis is Paris on the Prairie, not Bemidji of the South. Ours is Lake of the Isles, ringed by rollerbladers, not Lake of the Woods, ringed by wolf packs.

Clearly Mr. Jaeger was hallucinating, and that is that.

Until one Saturday in May on the street in front of our house.

Our teenaged son had just stepped out the front door in search of his own brand of evening urban wildness. As it was only the rim of sunset, the lad was not yet touched by the hallucinatory elixir of teenage evening freedom. So when he yelled for his mother with some urgency to come quickly to our front porch, she obeyed, particularly since he was mumbling words that sounded like, "There's a deer out here! On Clemence's lawn!"

The Clemences are our neighbors across the street. So, apparently, is a deer.

The deer stood still, head up, ethereal in a halo of dust raised by two years of street repaving. Bambi had grown up and come to the Big City.

Startled, the deer bounded down the Clemence lawn into the intersection, tore down the street half a block, then froze in the glare of headlights as a car turned into the street toward it. It quickly changed course and bounded onto the lawn of Debbie Gessner's house three doors away.

Dinner had broken up at the Gessner household and her guests were descending the front steps toward their cars.

Two of the guests just happened to be Indian spiritual men, one from South Dakota, the other from Red Lake, Minnesota. The third was Vine Deloria, Jr., Lakota attorney, scholar and writer of seminal books on Indian issues. They were on their way to take part in a healing ceremony in St. Paul. None appeared at all surprised to look up and encounter a deer on Debbie's front lawn in her urban neighborhood. They were no strangers to deer in all their fantastic incarnations.

The deer slowly followed the men up the avenue. As they stepped into their parked car, it slipped between two houses, and disappeared.

If Mrs. Coyote and the teenaged one can be believed, and they told me this story with breathless sincerity, then we have no choice but to believe Paul Jaeger as well.

I hope it's true. Wildness is another virtue we can add to the human variety in our vibrant urban neighborhood. That is a benefit of hallucinatory proportions.

Block Parties: A 'How To' Guide

(September 1989)

As I strolled through the neighborhood returning from a Sunday evening run, I was thinking about how burned out

I was from a long workweek. And how much of a pleasure it would be to get home and fix dinner and relax with the paper, which I had not yet read, and perhaps watch *60 Minutes*, and then maybe make a few fund-raising phone calls for a non-profit organization. I was savoring the gift of peace and quiet conferred on me by the absence of Mrs. Coyote and all the Little Coyotes, who were visiting family out of town.

A block from the house, I spied a neighborhood friend sitting on the screened porch of her house reading a book. I hadn't talked to her for several months. She didn't see me. Should I say hello, or pass on by to my peaceful dinner, paper, news and fund-raising?

"Hello Ann," I called. "Hello," she smiled, and we talked for a minute through the screen. She invited me in. Should I accept or rush home for the last half of *60 Minutes*?

I went in. As I cooled down on her porch with a glass of ice water, we spent a half-hour discussing each other's families and the grand political/social/ethical/ecological issues of the day. I finally got up, a bit stiff, and thanked her for the water. She thanked me for stopping in. Then I walked home.

What did that stop cost me? A lot. Time is money, money is time. I missed *60 Minutes* plus several phone calls.

What did I gain? Not much, as I am sure Ann will agree. We did not solve the ethical/social/political/ecological crises of the day, nor did we even agree whether we should pursue them idealistically or pragmatically. The information we exchanged about our children will not change their lives or ours.

And yet I'm glad I stopped. And that she invited me in. And that we talked.

This kind of gain is not measured in half-hour segments

of hard-hitting news and information. Nor is it measured in growth along the career path. It doesn't enhance our children's chances of attending the college of their choice, nor feed the cat, water the grass, call the plumber, wipe the counter, sweep the driveway, fix the car or paint the porch.

We just "caught up," playing our parts in the slow procession called neighborhood.

A more formal element in the process of neighborhood is the block party, and the two are linked.

Our welcome to this particular neighborhood was cemented by an invitation to a block party on Humboldt Avenue one block from us the year we moved in. That was fifteen years ago, and we still eagerly attend that gathering.

In the beginning, the Humboldt Avenue invitations were handwritten and distributed door to door by little Kelen and White kids. Now the invitations are laser-printed and distributed by big Kelen and White kids. But the rules are the same. Bring your own food and drink. Grills provided (as long as enough people lend their grills). What a wonderfully simple formula for catching up with old neighbors and meeting new ones while drinking and grilling on the side. Now no one need be strangers in their neighborhood.

For the last decade or so, I have advocated a party on our block since we have benefited so much from the next block's efforts.

Thanks to Humboldt Avenue, I have also learned the few other required procedures:

1) Call the city clerk. Ask for an application for a "Block Event" permit at least two weeks before the desired date. Send in fifteen dollars, plus the signatures of seventy-five percent of the households facing the affected street. On the

morning of the event, the Public Works Dept. will deliver barricades used to block automobile access to the street. They'll pick them up the following day.

2) Distribute leaflets along the blocks of your choice, giving street name of event, location, time, fee (if any), food type to bring, a rain date.

3) Prepare a communal dish.

4) Attend.

Number four often is the hardest part. All of us have higher priorities than neighborliness gnawing at our time, such as work and school and vacations to escape from work and school.

All true. So you may have to miss it. But if you do, attend every year you can.

Because the "low priority" benefits of block parties accrue as deep deposits in the community bank. These deposits pay invaluable interest in the form of a sense of belonging and a sense of place.

I am convinced that these payments have lifetime value; therefore, I advise everyone I know to throw such a party immediately upon moving to a new neighborhood—a block party if the area consists of private houses, otherwise an apartment "floor party" or "condo party." My mother started one of these in her retirement condominium in Florida, and it has become a much-anticipated annual event, the only occasion in her building where residents take the time to get to know each other.

This year our block finally threw its party. I pontificated on the subject for years, but Mrs. Coyote finally organized it.

Was our block party a success?

Well, the scheduled day was the only one in two weeks that threatened a torrential downpour. This was consistent with Mrs. C's expectations. She should be hired as a rain-maker. Every outdoor event she plans brings ferocious storms. However, it actually only sprinkled that day.

Did anyone show up? Yes, a good crowd, at least half of them new to us from the immediate two-block area.

Did we eat well? Of course. The loaves and fishes story is acted out at every block party.

Did we have a good time? Like all parties, this one passed too quickly, and I was able to talk at length to only a few of the new neighbors. One turned out to be an old acquaintance who had been living only a block away for over a year and I didn't know it.

Will we do it again? Of course. How obvious. A block party? It's so simple. Next year we will "catch up" again.

Thank you, Kelens and Whites, for the gift of inclusion fifteen years ago. Thank you, Mrs. Coyote, for finally getting it started on our block.

Now who is going to do it on yours? So that when you walk through your neighborhood, tired, burned out, alone, the opportunity for real human contact will be there in every house you pass. So you too can call, "Hello, Ann," through a screen. You too can receive a smile of recognition in return.

Post-Football Depression

(November 1989)

My son called long distance Monday night. He's 6'4" tall, a college graduate and is living in Boston. He has friends, a job, a girlfriend. But he was depressed. He needed to talk. So he called home.

The first voice he heard was that of Mrs. Coyote. Generally she is the one you want to reach when depressed. She dispenses wise balm on all major topics while I just mumble and fumble. She is sharp as a razor on the idiocies of men and women, cooking, politics and relationships of all kinds.

They talked for ten minutes or so, but she couldn't identify his problem.

Then it was my turn. I knew the answer before I picked up the phone. He was suffering from PFD. Post-Football Depression. I knew because I was suffering from it too.

We both had just witnessed on national TV the Minnesota Vikings lose to the inferior Philadelphia Eagles. By one point. And play lame, uninspired offense. And fumble twice. And make silly penalties. And otherwise bumble. It was a tormenting drama.

He needed to share his inexpressible angst. He certainly couldn't talk to his roommate. The guy grew up in Philadelphia. Even though the Eagles played the game like club-footed geese, they won it. Gloat City. His roommate is experiencing Post-Victory Elation, PVE, the symptoms of which include an unrealistic sense of superiority and invulnerability. Communicating across such an emotional gulf is like shouting across the Grand Canyon.

The Big Guy and I exchanged deep, plaintive moans. What is wrong with the Vikings? Why can't they get the offense going? Why have they suddenly developed fumblitis? Where is the spark? Why don't they use the new back more? Which coaches can we get rid of quickly? What kind of an idiot is the owner?

The questions spun out like a roll of toilet paper loose on the bathroom floor. No answers, just questions one after the other. Of course there are no answers for PFD, talk is all that matters. Post-game hotline.

All males in the family suffer from PFD. The Teenaged Coyote coped with his case by immediately crashing on the couch for two hours. Never mind he had his room to clean and homework to do, he was overcome with heaviness. His body wouldn't respond. His mind was dim. He couldn't get up. He was depressed.

I, on the other hand, leaped off the post-game couch with desperate, killing energy, and began barking orders like a Nazi lieutenant. Get moving, everybody! Sweep the floor! Dust the plants! I was tight as a fist, touchy as a sea urchin.

I had PFG, Post-Football Guilt. I was overdue to clean the house for the advancing Thanksgiving hordes and I knew it. Mrs. Coyote had been on my case all week. "The house is a shambles and your relatives are coming to stay. Get with the clean-up, Coyote. You don't have to watch this stupid football game every week."

Stupid game? Stupid game! Of course it's a stupid game. I know that. But I am a Football Fundamentalist, not open to argument based on reason or priorities. I watch the game because I have always watched the game, because that is what I do on Fall Sundays and we do not debate why I am watching the game, even in the face of Thanksgiving relatives and a house that looks like Mongol Hordes have camped inside, horses and all. I'll deal with it after the game.

Of course, she doesn't really expect a rational response. She's a non-believer, and loves to rub in her calm atheism. Her unanswerable questions drive me wild.

"Are the Vikings why you have been so miserable this fall?" she asks, broom in hand. "Are they the source of your spiritual crisis?" "Miserable?" I respond. "The Vikings are still 7-5 and leading the league! How could I be miserable?"

She's right, I am miserable. So are my sons. Does she finally understand the heartbreak of PFD? I doubt it.

Post-Football Depression mostly afflicts males, although women can catch it. Those who grew up in NFL communities are the most susceptible. I grew up next door to Green Bay, Wisconsin, football's Lourdes and Mecca. No more need be said.

My children grew up in Vikings country. The purple and white team that inhabits their murky, unformed souls has infected me as well. Even one of my two daughters has shown signs of the affliction. I am secretly elated. With this breakdown of the last great sexist division, I'll finally have a woman in the house with whom I can share my deepest emotional states.

When the team wins, I have an extra bounce in my step. I whistle uncontrollably. I break into spontaneous monologues. I have an unrealistically bright outlook. When the team loses, I'm sullen for days, or rage against the time I have wasted. All these symptoms drive Mrs. Coyote mad.

Oh well. The afflicted understand.

The Big Guy also called from Boston after last week's victory. His tone was buoyant, wanting to share his inexpressible joy. He does his best in Boston to contain quietly within him that vibrant burning firework of happiness called hometown victory. He may go out to a local bar and smile at the New England Patriot fans drooping over their beers. "Waiter, why is it so quiet in here? Oh, you mean the Patriots. Too bad. Well, I'm from Minnesota. We just won today. Buy a round on me."

Win or lose, we count on the phone ringing from a thousand miles away. Whether suffering PFD or PVE or PFG, he can only touch on important football feelings with another fan, a father who feels it too.

Coyote Goes Round the Bend

(December 1989)

At forty-five years old, I am halfway round my allotted planetary circuit, more or less. If I get Alzheimer's, I hope it will be less. If I get wisdom, I hope it will be more.

At this point on my circuit, I notice my priorities changing. No, not really changing, just expanding. Let me explain with a simple and I expect simple-minded metaphor.

A life is like a pebble dropped into a pool, surrounded by a series of concentric circles radiating out to the horizon. After forty-five years I'm starting to get a handle on what type of splash I am.

The first ring is family. That's a life's work, raising four children and tangling with the ferocious, bright-eyed Mrs.

Coyote while running with a pack of relatives, in-laws and friends.

The next ring is work. I've messed around in this one for a long time, often with a kind of circular tail chasing, until writing evolved into the core of what I do, and that (thank God) became reasonably settled.

For the last twenty years I have also put an enormous amount of energy into the next circle, community. We sought out the "intentional communities" of the early seventies, then discovered true community, called "neighborhood," in Minneapolis. For me community has always had a high priority, perhaps as a protest against the anomie of modern life, perhaps as an affirmation of my small town childhood, perhaps because of an intuitive sense of the value of interconnectedness.

The next ring is society—city, state, nations, cultures. Addressing social problems has been on my agenda for the past twenty years as well, becoming part of my daily work.

The next ring is planet Earth, the lessons of ecology and American Indian eloquence and stunning astronaut earth photographs all mocked by an increasing environmental mess. I've toiled at this one for twenty years as well, and Mother Earth is still up to her elbows in toxic rain and trash.

These necessary rings are each full of consuming passions, and passions that consume. One could live within any one of them for a lifetime.

However, as the rings have expanded and thinned over time, they have become more at one with the pool. As that process occurs, I have become restless again, begun to ask new questions.

What is the pool? And what is below its surface?

These days I am confronted by the question of religion.

Mrs. Coyote is no help in this matter. She suffers from what she calls PCD, Permanent Catholic Damage. That is the paradoxical affliction in which the politics and hierarchies of the Mother Church feel anachronistic and off-putting, yet no other religion, by definition, is the One True Church. So she chooses no formal religion, and seems happy with that decision, although she, not I, taught our children to say their prayers at night.

I was raised Congregationalist, a religion that seemed to me as a youth almost secular, a celebration of the coming of the Pilgrims, not of spirit. The Pilgrims do not turn me on. In fact, with my long interest in the many contributions of American Indians, they turn me off. Puritans introduced humorlessness and black clothing to North America, a cultural disaster from which the nation has yet to recover.

But I learned something valuable while sitting in that pew among the congregations of my youth. I learned the calming habit of ritual, such as singing in unison and putting money in the plate when it is passed, and sitting still while listening to a minister ruminate about something other than the daily round.

Of course, in those days my greatest interest *was* the daily round. Throughout many of the sermons of my childhood, I imagined I was bouncing a basketball off the church's Gothic arch supports. This mental exercise didn't improve my free-throw percentage with the DePere, Wisconsin Redbirds, but it did help me learn to sit still.

Perhaps it was the sitting still. Perhaps it was the Doxology, one of only two songs I can still sing by heart: "Praise God from whom all blessings flow." Perhaps it was the feisty family experience on Sunday mornings, with Dad riding herd when the family was moving too slowly getting ready for church. He was wise enough not to allow any dispensation for a sleepy boy lying on the soft living room rug reading the Sunday funnies, unable to move a muscle.

However I learned it, I now understand that an essential experience, now that I am ready to recall it, takes place *out* of the other circles—of self, family, neighborhood, job, society, environment, all so righteous and needy and consuming. It is the opportunity to address, in the common phrase, "the quiet place within us."

But is that place "within us"? Or is it in that pool, which carries all the other waves and yet is only rippled?

I don't have a clue. But I do have this urge. So now I venture into church whenever I get the chance. Which is not very often, since I run up against the many Sunday rituals by now firmly established in my other lives.

The ritual reading of the Sunday newspaper, now two of them, can take all morning, still beginning with the funnies. I am also the chef for the family's traditional Sunday breakfast. For twenty years I have prepared a steady supply of Dad's special Sunday pancakes topped with melted butter and yogurt and fruit and pure grade A amber maple syrup, not ersatz. Plus thick-sliced, home-smoked bacon. Plus freshly squeezed orange juice and fresh ground coffee. The family's mouths water every Sunday morning like Pavlov's dogs. So does mine. How can I stop now?

I can. These days the little Coyotes are now quite big, and love to sleep late. For them, Saturday night has eclipsed Sunday morning in ritual importance. Breakfast is now brunch. Great. I can sneak out.

I almost made it two weeks ago. Having read the paper and brewed the coffee while the family slept, I tiptoed out the back door toward the 10:30 a.m. service. In the garage, the sight of my daughter's bicycle reminded me that today was the annual neighborhood festival, started by my wife years before. The parade begins at noon! Aiee!! I dashed back inside and woke everybody up. Quick, we need to decorate bicycles and prepare for the parade!

Last Sunday looked free for sure. Then the phone rang. My friend Bill. What? You mean you have two extra tickets to the Packers-Vikings game on Sunday? My hometown team against my adopted Vikings? My son, a Vikings zealot who normally can't get out of bed till noon, will leap for this one! My sons and I have a powerful bonding experience through the rich ritual of fall football, despite our divided football loyalties.

So my attempted forays past the existing obligatory rings are mostly unsuccessful. Something always seems to come up. These are the facts of this stage of my life.

But as I contemplate the long slow fall of a stone through deep water, I am gaining some perspective. Clearly a life, however complicated and joyful, is only a ripple in a pool.

And I want to reach deeper into it. At least drag my fingers in the water. Feel the coolness. Taste the quiet. Do so without giving my yearning a name that will kill it, yet giving it enough of a vocabulary to recognize where in the quiet I am, where we all may be.

Where should I reach? I am fascinated by the Hopi of the American Southwest with their carefully balanced ceremonial cycles and the Cheyenne of the Northern Plains with their medicine wheel understanding and enlightened vision quests. I think those who dance round the moon to Wiccan goddesses have tapped a profound and liberating tradition. Judaism, with its passage of the Torah from generation to generation in an unbroken line across two millennia, fills me with awe and admiration. Zen Buddhism, with its discipline of meditation and its perplexing koan riddles, seems powerfully enlightening. On and on go the alternatives, certainly as good as the old Congregationalist one, maybe better. But I am not envious of any of them. One has to learn it in the bones. Which for me means the quietness I find in my old childhood church.

I badly want my children to join me there, even if they have to sulk up off the floor to discover the stillness. I do force them to attend, over their increasingly less bitter complaints, three times a year: Christmas, Easter and Thanksgiving. I know they will thank me for that at least when they are older.

As for the weekly ritual, my renewed commitment is too late for them, or too early. They will have to find their own still place. Perhaps they can do so without the Sunday morning bouncing ball memories I have. Perhaps they will find a fulfilling way to dance by the light of the moon. Or perhaps the Sunday morning rustle of newspapers and smell of maple syrup and frying bacon and family and neighborhood festivities will be enough. But I don't think so.

When I sensed that these textures and tastes weren't enough for me, when I wanted to find that still place inside me, I knew where to look. I went to the one place where I knew in my bones when to sit quietly, and when to stand and sing.

PART THREE

COYOTE COOLS OUT

1990–92

Is There Life after Earth Day?

(May 1990)

The warm glow of Earth Day is over, and the cold light of daily ecological commitment is upon me.

Up early with the cool morning breezes, I hear my neighbor's sprinkler whooshing. It has been whooshing for days. I growl at his wastefulness.

As I take a cold shower I try to remember all the Earth Day resolutions I made. Cold water is part of environmentally responsible showering, but my shivering cuts off morning meditations.

Breakfast time. Toast or bread? Cold-pressed coffee or fresh perked? I sell out on both counts. Hot toast *and* hot coffee. Mmmmmm.

Read the paper with stories of global warming on the front page. The temperature is expected to rise to eighty-six degrees today. The humidity is already enough to dissolve a whole body in hydrochloric tears. And this is April. Ouch.

Our youngest child trips down the stairs like she's tripping through the tulips. She eats breakfast, assembles her gear and trots off early to the second grade school bus. The school is only seven blocks away and she takes a bus? I growl as I smell the exhaust.

Our teenaged son stumbles down the stairs, fresh from his hot shower, his ratty backpack shedding broken pencils and shreds of paper. He snatches the newspaper to review important ecological information—baseball scores and music reviews—then races out the door.

He's back. Can't find his car keys. Runs back upstairs. Down again. Frustration. Up again. He finds them. He's off again.

He's back. Car won't start. His 1974 VW bug is parked on a nearby hill because the battery is dead, so he rolled it and popped the clutch, his usual procedure, but it wouldn't start. Darn, he says, that hill worked last time.

I offer to help. I step out the back door and find his car straddling both lanes of the street. I hunker down in the humidity and push him faster and faster down the block. Still no start. Did he turn the key on? I ask. Oops, he says. I push him down the next hill. Puffs of smoke emerge from his tailpipes. Contact. He's off to school.

I am perspiring. Wait a minute, why doesn't *he* take a school bus? Uncool, uncool.

To cool myself, I step into the garage to gaze upon my ecologically correct commuting vehicle: a bicycle. I am so excited. Now that spring is here (or is it summer?), I can begin the bicycle commuting season.

I work downtown, a ten-minute car ride, fifteen-minute bus ride, twelve-minute bicycle ride. Of the three, only the bicycle does not produce greenhouse gases.

My bicycle is especially outfitted for the purpose of commuting. Over the winter I installed a large wire basket on the front, the kind we all had as kids but is hard to find these days. It is big enough to hold three full bags from the grocery store, or my regular commuting stuff.

I purchased the basket because of an unhappy experience as a bicycle commuter last year.

Last year I installed a rack over my back wheel, the kind

that has a platform about four inches wide and twelve inches long to which you fasten stuff with bungee cords. Very trendy.

The rack proved to have a fundamental flaw that could not be overcome by whatever web of bungees I tried. My briefcase fell off. The good news is that no bus ran over it, although several came close more than once.

Let me tell you about this briefcase. It contains about forty pounds of stuff. I always carry forty pounds of stuff, although I often don't do anything like forty pounds of work at home. Somehow after dinner and reading bedtime stories and kicking butt about homework, work energy is a little harder to find than when I left the office.

But if I don't bring home forty pounds of stuff, that will be the day I have the energy to do forty pounds of work. I must be prepared.

Into the bicycle's basket this morning I place the forty-pound briefcase, a thermos of fresh-brewed coffee, a lunch packed in a recycled ice cream bag, my sport coat neatly folded, my tie, my raincoat. It all fits. I am triumphant, even though it is by now 8:15 a.m., later than I like to leave. I pedal off toward town.

Six blocks later my pedal falls off. Actually the whole crank falls off.

Cursing and perspiring, I set the kickstand and attempt, with no tools whatsoever, to reattach the crank. In the process, the top heavy bicycle falls over, spilling out my briefcase, my raincoat, my sport coat, my tie, my thermos, my lunch.

I load everything back into the basket, including the crank, and walk the bike back home, uphill most of the way.

Muttering, I unlock the door and ask my wife if I can put

my disabled bicycle into her energy-efficient van and take it to the alternative bicycle repair shop six blocks away. She is on the phone but nods No, her van is clean and my bike is not. So I put the one-cranked bicycle into the trunk of my less-than-energy-efficient car, where it hangs out the maw of the trunk and over the bumper. I drive slowly to the bike shop. The sign on the door says *Open at 10 a.m.*

I drive back home. As I take the bike out of the trunk, I notice that the wire basket has rubbed against the car's paint above the taillight and now there is no paint above the taillight.

I put the crank into the basket and re-park the bicycle in the garage and stumble, hot and greasy, to my car. I notice that two of its tires are badly distended. Earth Day guidelines are very clear on this: inadequate tire pressure leads to poor gas mileage, an area in which my car is already suspect. I drive to the gas station (near the bike repair shop where I'd just been) and overfill the tires.

Now it is time to drive to work, where I arrive an hour late.

Tonight I'll drive the bike to the repair shop, if I get home before it closes.

And tonight I *will* have to get out the forty-pound briefcase because I'm an hour behind in my work.

Well, there is always tomorrow to be ecologically correct. Tomorrow I'll get that energy-efficient bicycle back on the road. And get my son out of his cheap and evil car. And get my daughter to walk to school. I can hardly wait to educate them in proper ecological consciousness. Unless it rains or gets too hot. Then I'll climb into my old automobile and turn on the AC.

Help, Parent Abuse in Progress!

(June 1990)

When the second grade class was assigned a research paper, our daughter picked "dolphins." That was two weeks ago. Friday she announced that the paper was due on Monday and she wasn't finished. She panicked.

Our oldest daughter, home from college, agreed to help. She guided the second grader through the rigors of research in the Encyclopedia Britannica, the World Book, and *Dolphin Log,* the newsletter of the Cousteau Society.

The second grader cooperated reluctantly, surly that she had to write this, her first research paper, at all. Our house was much disturbed by her moaning and other noises of a negative nature. She focused on the paper only when a powerful motivating force was brought into play.

It seems she was aware that Disney's *The Little Mermaid* was due to arrive at video stores that day. She loved *The Little Mermaid*, sang all the songs, knew all the characters, and felt a compelling need to study it over and over again.

She insisted that I run out and rent the movie immediately. I said I would rent it for her, but only when her paper was done. She said, rent it today and she would watch it tomorrow. I said only if she finished her paper would I rent it.

Sunday she penciled in the last sentence just as Mrs. Coyote and I went out for a rare Sunday evening obligation.

Upon returning, the second grader was in bed asleep. "One thing," said the college daughter. "She went to bed unhappy, saying that she still didn't like her paper."

Uh oh. A recipe for morning trouble, with which we had much experience. Best to be prepared.

I located the research paper instructions written on a

scrap of pink construction paper in our daughter's second grade folder. The teacher required a title page, two pages of text and a list of references.

I looked at the assembled work lying on the kitchen table. The cover had a wonderful drawing of two frolicking dolphins. The two pages of text described the number of dolphin teeth, their diet of fish and squid, and their use of an item on the front of their head called a "melon" for "echolocation." The word was spelled correctly. The last sheet of paper listed all the references, also spelled correctly. I was a proud and relieved papa.

Only the title page was missing, and that could be prepared in a minute or two during breakfast. This was going to be the finest second grade research paper in the history of the universe!

The next day dawned sunny and clear. After my early breakfast, I bounded up the stairs to wake my daughter. I brought her the new puppy, which she loved. I also brought her the dolphin report to help her begin her morning with the knowledge that it was only one minute away from perfection.

She loved the puppy licking her face, and cuddled him. She scowled at the report.

"I don't like the drawing," she said. "It's a great drawing," I said. "I don't like it," she said.

Unfortunately, we had seen this kind of behavior often in her six years. My strategy was to confront her right away with her anxieties so that by the time she was dressed and through her cereal and banana she would have dropped into rational focus. It had worked many times before.

But during today's cereal and banana, she said the drawing still didn't look right. "OK, OK," I said, "don't take the drawing. It's not required anyway. Just write DOLPHINS and your name on a blank sheet of paper for the title sheet and you're done!"

"I don't like the drawing," she responded. "I can't go to school." "But you have to go to school." "I can't go to school." "Why not?" "Because the drawing isn't right."

In the meantime Mrs. Coyote was leaning on the kitchen counter making a peanut butter and jelly sandwich for our daughter's school lunch. She has a miraculous touch with the Little One's legendary intransigence but had been quite sick the night before and was green and wobbly this morning. Although she normally handles school bus departures, I had volunteered to leap into the breach.

The Little One began crying hard, "I can't go to school, I can't go to school." "Look," I reasoned, "you hate to miss the bus. You hate worse to be driven to school and arrive separately. You cannot stay home; no one will be here. It is now eight minutes to the bus, plenty of time to get ready."

More tears. Higher pitched wails. I looked at my wife, who was eyeing the sink with a green half-smile.

The Little One's best friend came to pick her up for school at the back door. Usually her presence helped, but not today. More wails. Her friend left so she didn't miss the bus herself. Our daughter was of course embarrassed that she was seen wailing by her friend, thus wailed all the more. I prepared her red school bag, putting in her lunch and her regular school folder. Cleverly, I showed her that I was adding her research paper. "Don't worry about the title page. The teacher will love the paper," I reassured her, certain it was true. Even higher pitched wails.

Three minutes to the school bus. I told her that either she

leave for the bus stop NOW or I would have to drive her to school. Which would it be? (My psychology here was that she would recognize her double bind, choose the lesser of two evils, and quickly get it together for the bus. Hey, I wasn't crazy. This strategy had also worked before). Instead, immense freaked-out screams accompanied floods of tears.

OK, it's DAD time! "You cannot stay home for no reason. You will be driven or take the bus. This is the end of the line." I took her kicking and screaming down the back stairs toward the bus, hoping that this disruptive movement would inspire her to face reality. Pathetic high-pitched screams and sobs. I stopped in the back yard and tried to hug her into calming down. She fought away and screamed that she *wouldn't take* the bus and *wouldn't drive* in the car. I pulled her further by the arm into the driveway and sat her down just across from the car door. The bus would pass by ten feet from us. This was her last chance to calm down and get into the bus line, which I knew she preferred. Murderous high-pitched screams, "No, no, Daddy, no, noooo!!!!"

Out of the corner of my eye, I noticed people going to work looking into the driveway where my daughter and I sat nose to nose in pathos. Then the school bus drove past.

I imagined at this point flinging her into the car, strapping her in, driving to school with her screaming and thrashing, dragging her into the school and into the school room, handing her over to the teacher and leaving. Sound cruel? Truth be known, my wife and I had used this desperate procedure more than once before—always with the result that she had a happy day at school, returning home with a bounce in her step.

Yet I found it difficult to muster the necessary enthusiasm for this draconian approach. However, the unstated alternative—staying home alone brooding in her room—was unacceptable given my wife's green condition. We both faced each other, lost in a dark, depressing dead-end box.

The Little One continued to scream in the driveway. Then, from nowhere, rationality broke through. She cried, "I want my Mommy!"

Analysis. This was the first time all morning she had said anything for which there was a possible affirmative answer, not a Catch 22. I stepped inside the house and gingerly inquired after Mommy's health.

Mommy, it turned out, had repaired to the farthest corner of the bedroom, not wanting to complicate current matters in her green condition. She had heard the screams. She wobbled back downstairs as the Little One ran in behind me and collapsed sobbing in her mother's arms. The Green One carried her up to bed for mutual recuperation.

Our college daughter and teenaged son bumbled downstairs and into the kitchen in response to the commotion. At which point the doorbell rang. My son got it, as I was pacing in the kitchen like a caged cat and late for work to boot. I heard two male voices, Jehovah's Witnesses, I figured. My son talked to them while I stuffed my briefcase for a harried departure. He came back to the kitchen with a quizzical smile on his face.

"The police," he said, "investigating a complaint of child abuse."

Child abuse? I answered. CHILD abuse! How about PARENT ABUSE instead?!?!!

My son had assured the policemen that the commotion was only his little sister not wanting to take her homework to school. They smiled and retired to their car, on to more weighty crimes.

Still, I imagined our pathetic drama adding another item to

that day's blotter at Minneapolis' Fifth Precinct: "Investigated complaint of child abuse on Girard Avenue. Dismissed as a case of homework anxiety."

The facts of this story are not pretty for anyone involved except the police.

As parents of four children, we well know that every child has his or her own behavioral peculiarities. In addition, we as parents have our own stark failings. This particular child has always had massive separation anxiety—from home and especially from Mommy—even though at school she has happy days and wins spelling bees and can write "echolocation" without a second thought. The most effective resolution of the separation problem has been to make sure she has enough time in the morning to overcome her fears and still make the school bus. That strategy certainly didn't work today.

Sometime after my departure, the Green One was able to calm the second grader and get her to school an hour late accompanied by a fresh dolphin drawing and a precisely printed title sheet. The Little One returned from school that afternoon cheerful as a chickadee.

Prior to my leaving the house for work, rattled and bedraggled, I called directory assistance for 800 numbers. I asked for the Parent Abuse Hotline. There was no such thing, the operator reported. "Too bad," I said. "I could have used it."

Maybe I should be happy I avoided arrest.

Turf Wars

(November 1990)

Jim and Cindie and Casey Smart were feeling settled this summer, so they decided to landscape the yard. Their house backs up on an abandoned railroad right-of-way where trains once rumbled through the neighborhood. The Smarts wanted to create a buttress of civility against that backdrop of towering weedy growth. They built a wall of boulders and fieldstones inside of which, as the crowning measure, they laid fresh Minnesota sod. They stood together in the sunset at the end of August, Jim hugging Cindie, Cindie hugging Jim, both hugging the toddler Casey who was hugging the dog Asa, and exhaled a collective sigh of pleasure. The wall was handsome, the sod green and smooth as a pool table. They set out the sprinklers and went to bed in utter assurance of joy in the world, in spite of war ravaging the Mideast and a budget crisis in Washington. At home, life was green and in control.

The next morning the fresh sod was folded over and brown at the edges. What unspeakable vandals had terrorized their peaceful nest?

Jim's investigation revealed that the turf was folded lengthwise from the edges. From the dim recesses of their small-town memories, the Smarts called up ancestral images of a creature with such a turf-folding fetish.

Raccoons!

Raccoons! Raccoons must be hunting for fat worms and grubs under the moist carpet of sod. Raccoons were coming for dinner but refusing to put away the napkins!

Raccoons are hardly new residents of the neighborhood. They have recycled our garbage for years. The Smarts' 160-pound dog Asa bore psychological scars of a recent raccoon encounter.

He had jerked his leash out of Cindie's hand to chase a raccoon family ambling along the railroad tracks. The raccoons were openly disdainful toward this hurtling ravenous barking giant dragging an empty leash behind him. They unhurriedly repaired to the nearby lagoon and jumped in. Asa followed, whereupon the raccoons swiftly turned on him and jumped on his head, attempting to drown him. This is a raccoon tactic well known to country creatures, but alas apparently new to *canis familiaris urbanis*, the fire hydrant's friend. Jim manfully waded into the muck, bringing Asa home alive and unbowed but bitten all over his head.

So the Smarts knew about raccoons. But what to do? They re-rolled the sod, set the sprinkler and went to work, hoping the problem would go away.

The next day the turf was folded. Again they unfolded it, set the sprinkler and went to work. That night Jim woke up several times and flashed the area with a halogen beam. Nothing. The next morning the turf was folded, brown at the edges.

Time for a counterattack. A call to Animal Control revealed that if the Smarts were to live-trap any raccoons, the city would dispose of them.

So the Smarts rented a live trap, twelve bucks the week. It seemed small by comparison with the massive brutes that chewed on Asa, but was of clever design. Put a dose of peanut butter on a paddle in the center of the trap. The creature enters to eat the peanut butter—one of humankind's most irresistible foods, little Casey's favorite—and the doors slam shut at both ends. Excellent.

The next morning the trap was sprung. The peanut butter was gone. The trap was bare. The turf was folded.

The next day the same, and the day after that. Casey was beginning to cry out for the missing peanut butter, her favorite food now reserved for a higher purpose.

The Smarts finally figured out the problem. The raccoons were springing the trap, reaching in to take the peanut butter from the outside, then polishing off the feast with a dessert of grubs and worms from under the turf.

The Smarts are smart. They took leftover landscaping stones and piled them all around the trap so the vandals couldn't reach in from the outside. The next morning the peanut butter was gone, the turf folded. Seems they had piled the stones so close the trap couldn't spring. Jim re-piled the stones.

In two and a half weeks, they caught one baby raccoon. Jim took back the trap. The rental man smiled.

Jim decided to call in the heavies, the animal experts at the University of Minnesota. They advised spreading a chemical that kills the attractive worms and grubs. However, they added, don't let any kids or pets or other living organisms use the yard for weeks. The stuff is toxic as plutonium. That killed that suggestion.

Co-workers at Jim's office noticed the growing wildness around his eyes. One chimed in with a helpful folk remedy. Spread human hair around the yard, he said. Smart's barber had heard the same thing, and gave Jim a bag of hair. However, he added, he had also heard that you have to replenish the hair after a rain. For some reason hair no longer works when wet.

That night Smart was in his backyard, flashlight in his mouth, eyes glowing, lips curled, spreading shreds of human hair around the perimeter of his turf with wild abandon.

Dawn rolled over downtown high rises and urban lakes and the neighborhood grid inhabited with an awake, alert Jim Smart rubbing his hands and watching for folds in the telltale turf. Eureka! The lawn dawned flat and green as a polo field.

Before he left for work, he set the sprinkler. The next morning the turf was folded. The sprinkler!

The Smarts' choice was finally clear. Sprinkle and live with folded brown turf. Or stop sprinkling and live with flat brown turf.

A third choice came to mind. Take a vacation.

When they returned several days later, the sod was moist and green and flat. The vandalism had miraculously ceased.

Jim and I considered three explanations for the raccoons' surprising retreat. One, the turf had finally rooted and would no longer fold. Two, the raccoons had become lethargic with the growing October chill. Three, the raccoons tired of the turf rolling game when the delightfully responsive human audience was no longer in attendance. Who needs grubs and worms in a neighborhood of plentiful garbage cans? But a rollicking laugh to end a night's work, now that makes raccoon life worth living.

It is now late October. The Smarts' sod grows smartly with only a few remnant brown patches as scars from the ordeal. The dog too has healed, albeit with a twitch. Jim and Cindie, chastened from the unexpected rigors of urban living, have regained their smiles. They again go out at night and tell stories.

We reserve our deepest sympathies for Casey, the toddler. Her entire supply of peanut butter disappeared without a trace that terrible fall. She had to eat mashed broccoli and turnips until the raccoons stopped laughing and went home.

Turning Twenty-one with Champagne and Bombs

(January 1991)

How do parents celebrate the arrival of a daughter at twenty-one, the long-awaited "legal age?" And what should they do when that day happens to occur at the onset of a war?

We had invited our daughter to dinner with several friends of hers from work. While driving to the restaurant, we heard on the radio that United Nations forces initiated the bombing of Iraq to force Saddam Hussein to roll back his invasion of Kuwait.

At the restaurant, my wife gave our daughter a garland of flowers for her hair. She smiled in her flowered crown above her vintage 1940's rayon dress that coordinated remarkably with her cowboy boots.

Her passage to adulthood had been rough, with major battles and protracted, moody uncertainties in the adolescent wars. Yet here she was, eclectically stylish, wreathed in flowers in a fine restaurant ordering champagne as an adult.

It is bizarrely subversive that the last major stepping stone into American adulthood is the legal drinking of alcohol. Bizarre because everyone knows the drinking age limit is arbitrary. Subversive because the law is routinely mocked. And yet somehow right because, absurd and painful as the waiting process is, at least there is *something* to mark the end of the ordeal of adolescence. Legal access to bars is no Holy Grail but at least it represents some last threshold before one fully enters the adult community's range of freedoms and responsibilities.

Still, I wish American culture provided far more serious

and appropriate rites of passage into adulthood. Parents need some valuable secret that we could give her now to initiate her into the corridors of the world's wisdom. But the only secret we still firmly hold encompasses the immensity and limits of adulthood itself, a world that can only be experienced.

We know that adulthood means giving back as well as taking. It means confronting fear in the pit of your stomach, mastering it and feeling the power of that mastery help you confront the next fear more easily until new challenges become eager enthusiasms.

Adulthood is full of joys less intense than those of childhood or adolescence but that last much longer, until on days like today they stretch deep into the future and twenty-one years into the past.

Perhaps our family's coming of age ritual should have included sitting down together and reading *Anna Karenina*, that Fort Knox of secrets of the human heart and mind and spirit. Why didn't I think of that before?

Such questions and reflections welled up in me as I looked at my daughter's brilliant smile in that restaurant on the occasion of her twenty-first birthday. We toasted her life to come.

Yet our birthday table conversation was troubled by the terrible thunder of American jets bombing Iraq for the first time that night. And so we wondered not only about coming of age rituals for younger Americans but about the quality of wisdom resident in the adult community she had just joined. Perhaps older political leaders should all sit down together and read *War and Peace*. Its bloody lessons could be a useful initiation for them, just as we toast our daughter into the vagaries of the adult world, bombs and champagne and all.

The Funeral File

(March 1991)

I keep a file at my office marked, "Funeral, Mine." Into it I toss scraps of paper holding ideas related to this ultimate event of my lifetime. Am I crazy or morbid? Neither.

Anything which affects everybody can't be bad. Equality, equity, fairness are all good words, not bad ones. So too with death, I figure. Name one person who has successfully avoided it. OK, name more than one. See. Death is a part of life.

So I am looking forward to death, or at least I'm infernally curious about it. Where does life's last great adventure lead?

None of this enthusiasm should imply that I am seeking it out prematurely. It does mean that I am beginning to plan my own funeral. I see the occasion—the end of a reasonably lengthy life—as a fine occasion for a community celebration.

Not everyone sees funerals this way. Some want theirs somber, a time of closed coffins and cold cuts. I understand. Tragedies, God knows, are tragedies.

My demise, obviously, will not be a tragedy. More like a comedy.

I sometimes wonder if I should attend my funeral propped up in the coffin, a flower in my lapel, a grin painted on my face, a fresh application of aftershave on my chin, some rouge sprayed on my cheeks to replace the color lost when my heart stopped pumping. If I do, don't try to dance with me. But that, of course, was wise advice during my life as well.

But whether or not I'm physically present in such a fashion—Mrs. Coyote, should she post-decease me, will never be convinced such attendance is desirable—I insist on good dance music, good food, good speeches, great poetry and the unveiling of one or two sculptures and commemorative scrolls. That's not too much to ask.

Some of you might feel such an exit performance excessive and wasteful. That's why I keep my own funeral file. I don't want you in charge.

Nor do I want some child or grandchild piping up at the last minute insisting instead on a small family gathering around dry flowers and dry food, incinerating me and providing charitable donations to useful organizations with the saved expense. Over my dead body, so to speak. I gave when I was alive.

To prevent such misunderstandings, I keep the file.

Who else should have such a file? You should, unless you are the One for whom an end is not in the cards. Everybody else needs one. Since death is open to all, funeral planning is open to all. I die, therefore I plan.

When should you start the file? As soon as the idea of death doesn't scare you. I started mine in my early forties.

Don't wait too long. You must get your planning underway before strokes, heart attacks, Alzheimer's Disease or muggers sneak up and whack your cerebellum. After that you get nasty, bitter, frustrated and drool on your shoes. Then it's too late. You will have forgotten your good intentions and those around you will remember only your bad moods.

I keep putting fresh notes into my funeral file. A song I like. A quotation I find stunning and to the point. A poem that moves my heart. A sketch for a suitable monument of remembrance.

My current sketch shows a tall Corinthian column on top of which howls a marble coyote. I added several benches around the plot for wanderers to sit and contemplate the

"Urban Coyote Column" and wonder: What the hell is *that* all about?

I love to take the children to visit Lakewood Cemetery. It is Minneapolis's first and still best sculpture garden, open to the public free of charge dawn to dusk. We particularly marvel at the romantic statue of a Greek maiden marking the plot of the Gluek family, well remembered if long departed brewers. The woman holds a rose in her hands. Against the backdrop of her gray granite hands and the folds on her gray granite robe, the rose is red. Startlingly red. Impossibly red.

Some of my more shy family members crave Quakerlike simplicity, quietly hoping I will ask for deathbed donations to the Nature Conservancy, public education and Vikings season tickets. All of these are worthy causes. But life is about much more than parks, schools and football. It's about community.

Did I forget to mention that you are all invited to my funeral? Be there or be square. Sing with gusto the lyrics of that great song the title of which I can't remember right now. Recite as well the lilting wisdom of William Stafford's poem to his wife—I can't remember the title of that one either. But the titles are not lost. They are written on scraps of paper somewhere in the funeral file.

Listen. Don't you hear the music and poetry? Don't you feel like dancing in the grass? Don't you see a tall marble statue howling in the moonlight, crying in the rain?

The funeral file. What a great way to plan for the rest of your life.

Tulips Do Not
Spring Happiness Make

(April 1991)

One of the joys I have as a Minnesotan is trumpeting the virtues of our state. When I travel, or when friends visit here, I am a veritable Canadian goose of obnoxious and persistent honking. Great business climate. Great educational system (oh yeah, you tried Detroit? Chicago? DC? LA?). Best parks system. Best cultural climate. Great sports scene. Superb higher education. Insignificant commutes (even without light rail). Ten thousand lakes. Ten thousand therapies. Progressive government (oh yeah, you tried Detroit? Chicago? DC? LA?). A host of excellent restaurants, where one can now expect espresso. The best caramel rolls. The best public radio and TV. Shall I go on?

They nod, clearly impressed. Then they throw me their version of the 110-mile-per-hour Dave Stewart fastball. What about the winter?

I am totally prepared for this question. I swat it back high over the fence with my version of the Dave Winfield (a Minnesota boy) swing.

The winter, I say, is wonderful.

Yes, it is cold, but the days are 65 percent sunny, dry and crystal clear, the snow white and clean. The spirit is uplifted by these virginal reflections. We do not huddle in gloomy winter humidity with constant runny noses. Nor do we suffer winter mudslides or droughts or floods.

We bask in fresh cleanliness. We frolic in our parks like animated Bruegel paintings of delighted skaters and cross-country skiers in the thrall of perfect aerobics. Both

NordicTrak® and Rollerblade® are Minnesota companies, I tell them. They are agog.

The Minnesota winter, I conclude as their jaws drop to their ties or cleavage, is ennobling and spectacular. I wish they could join us.

This truth provides an antidote to the common national perception of our winter. Southerners (everybody from Iowa down) imagine Minnesota as a state-sized storage locker for venison haunches. Executive recruiters cannot get people to move here because of our winter. The refusers are benighted, and so I delight in my winter therapy.

Fortunately, there is a question Southerners don't ask, and therefore I don't feel obliged to answer. What about the spring?

Minnesota's spring is a killer.

The 80-degree weekend two weeks ago was a major April fool's joke, replaced now by cold and drizzle. Not funny. In April Minnesota's citizens stalk the state like our spring flowers: instead of proud fragrant beauties, we are deformed, stunted and surly. We cannot believe what is happening to us. Instead of tiptoeing through the tulips, we are stomping through the slush.

T. S. Eliot must have been a Minnesotan. "April is the cruelest month," he stated without caveat. Look in our masochistic gardens if you don't believe him.

The Minnesota tulip is one of the most abused species on the planet. The life cycle of a Minnesota tulip is measured in minutes. A bulb responds to an unreasonably early heat wave by pushing up a bloom, only to have it crushed by snow, sleet, hail or all three. Tulips should apply for legal protection against transplantation to our soil. If unsuccessful in court, they should insist upon heated and air-conditioned covers over individual bulbs as protection against spring's outrageous vagaries, at least until the weather stabilizes (possibly around late June although nobody can say for sure); otherwise, back to Holland.

Daffodils resist Minnesota's phony spring blandishments a bit longer, thus lessening the abusive relationship. But they don't last long. Crocuses do best, as they are shy and hug the ground, basically expecting abuse by unseasonably sharp snow crystals. They are the Lutherans of spring flowers, and needless to say are not showy.

What Minnesota's spring flowers do show in their bruised, abused blossoms, we Minnesotans know in our hearts. Just as Minnesota's winter is a tonic for the soul, Minnesota's spring is murder for the psyche. It comes in like a lion and sticks around like a hyena.

I am writing this in the midst of four days of cold rain. Perhaps later in the year I will look back on this season with some fondness; say in July when the thermometer claws toward 100 degrees and the humidity rises toward a corrosive 99 percent. (Fortunately few ask about our summers either.) But for now, I think I will declare myself a tulip, fade quickly from the garden and retire to my dark basement in protest against the harshness of the Minnesota spring. You who stay above ground, watch out for tornadoes. Call me when it's time for the State Fair, fall and winter.

Coyote Joins the Church

(June 1991)

So there I was in the back row of Plymouth Congregational Church on Sunday, the second of June in the year of our Lord 1991. I had somehow extricated myself from the usual Sunday morning impediments—my wife's persistent agnosticism, the children's lethargy, the kitchen's coffee aroma, two newspapers to read and the stifling humidity outside. As I dressed hurriedly for church, I debated whether or not to wear socks. The day promised to be hot as Hades. No one should notice their absence, since I was on a personal spiritual journey that sallied forth just fine from the rearmost pew.

At the last minute I added colorful socks to the slightly wrinkled tan pants, the bright red tie and blue seersucker sport coat pulled from the back of the closet. My freshly showered hair rose like a haystack halo above my shaggy salt and pepper beard.

Good thing I dressed up. This was going to be a Sunday to remember.

Only a bit late, I glided into the back pew and glanced at the bulletin, from which a pink insert fell harmlessly to the floor. I noticed that in addition to the usual service components, today included a reception of new members. "New members," I whistled to myself, "is that something I could do today?"

Flashback. After several years of irregular attendance at Plymouth, last fall I made the decision to formally join the church. I found the sermons of Minister Vivian Jones enlightening, the music inspiring, the building stable, the ambiance peaceful.

In addition to such spiritual concerns, I was facing two pragmatic issues. I have a daughter approaching marriageable age. Second, at 47, I need to add additional detail to the plans for my funeral. A church is a place where both sacred ceremonies can be performed.

So I attended a new member orientation meeting at Plymouth Church last September. I listened as Reverend Jones related the history of Congregationalism and laid out the membership requirements. What I remember now of that meeting is some surprising Congregational history (the tradition is that ministers are considered teachers; Congregationalists founded Harvard College) and that a handshake in full view of the congregation is the sole ritual of new membership. I was ready to take that shake.

However, on the Sunday appointed for my official introduction to the congregation, I was called out of town on business.

I missed the next induction Sunday two months later, and the next, and the next. Business trips, neighborhood festivals, football games and family camping trips all made their insistent weekend claims.

For nine months these conflicts arose.

Initially, a diligent church secretary called regularly to ask if I would be attending the next induction ceremony. I earnestly intoned that I would. Finally she gave up the chase, no doubt believing that I was yet another member of my feckless generation unable to commit.

Meanwhile, on the random Sundays I did attend services, I now suffered a spiritual indignity whenever the "friendship" pads were passed up and down the aisle. Should I identify myself as a "member" or "visitor" in the boxes provided? I felt I was no longer merely a visitor, as I had been attending sporadically for several years and had "passed" the requisite membership orientation. Still I was not yet an official member. I often marked *both* boxes, an unsatisfying compromise I did not look forward to continuing into the fall.

So there I sat this humid Sunday in June with an opportunity to resolve my dilemma. However, I worried that I was not sure I remembered all the procedural details discussed at that membership meeting so long ago. Was there something more than a handshake required—a call and response, a breakfast meeting, a red carnation, a nametag?

I decided to handle the situation thusly: If the new members, when called from the pulpit, rose as a group, that would be a signal that I had forgotten some organizing event or procedure and therefore should sit tight, waiting for my random attendance to turn up the next such opportunity. On the other hand, if the new inductees sat scattered throughout the congregation, that would indicate to me that Congregational informalism and my memory were intact and only a simple handshake was required. I would then rise and join the others at the altar.

When Reverend Jones's call came from the pulpit, the new inductees rose from throughout the congregation. I rose and followed them forward.

They lined up in a semicircle facing the pulpit. I joined them on one end, smiling broadly at my decision. However, a glance down the line of my fellow inductees revealed red carnations and name tags as far as the eye could see. Oh oh. I have missed some special preparation after all. Should I turn back?

Fate placed me next to an old neighborhood friend, Barrs Lewis. "Barrs," I whispered, "do we have some text to recite?" "No," he whispered back, "but what the hell are you doing here?" I whispered that I had attended the class nearly a year ago, etc., etc., and he whispered whew, he thought

I might have been a Baptist or something and just popped up as the spirit moved me. I asked about the carnation and nametag. He whispered something about an organizational meeting prior to the service and that the new members' names were listed in the bulletin (so that's what that pink sheet was all about!). We turned our faces forward as Rev. Jones launched his remarks over our heads into the sea of the congregation, remarks that I now feared did not include me.

What to do? Turning back could be read by the two thousand eyes of the congregation behind me as a sign that, upon further reflection, I had decided not to become a member after all. On the other hand, staying in front was growing ever more uncomfortable. Although I now silently applauded my decision to wear socks, I faulted the choice of the blue seersucker sport coat, which I suddenly remembered had a mysterious orange stain in the middle of the back. Would the congregation view the stain as some sort of seersucker stigmata and fall on their knees in awe? More likely, they would rise up in a chorus of boos and nays over my rumpled and unaccountable appearance. Finally, I opined to myself with some relief, they would do neither. These are, after all, Congregationalists, for whom tolerance is a central doctrine.

Throughout this internal conversation, Reverend Jones radiated over our heads inspiring words about the church as community. I noticed that he also saw out of the corner of his eye my surprising presence. He appeared unruffled, but the two assistant ministers seated behind him suggested with their raised and mobile eyebrows a deeper concern. Was I a derelict who stumbled in to demand free wine?

Finishing his remarks, Rev. Jones descended from the pulpit and approached the semicircle of eager applicants plus one mendicant. Fortunately, he began at the applicant end.

He shook hands and welcomed each of the shiny, well-scrubbed new members by name, reading, I could now see, from the nametags. I wore no nametag. Oh oh. How would he know my name?

On this subject I had some cause for optimism. Over the years of my spotty attendance, Rev. Jones and I had enjoyed a few introductory encounters and even exchanged a letter or two. Now that I think of it, I had failed to return his prized volume of the Welsh poet R. S. Thomas's *Selected Poems* which he had lent me last October with the proviso that I please keep it only one month. (I can explain—I was actually reading the poems, good poems require absorption, where does the time go, etc.). On the other hand, that inadvertence might place me somewhere in his memory. Would he use this occasion to ask for the book's return, or had he forgotten the whole episode, including me?

Rev. Vivian Jones finally reached the last place in line. My place. "Surprise!" I whispered sheepishly. "Mr. James Lenfestey," he intoned with a firm handshake, "I welcome you into the community of Plymouth Congregational Church." He winked. I winked back.

On the second of June 1991, a deal was struck before the congregation of Plymouth Congregational Church in Minneapolis that was far more momentous than anybody could have expected that morning. Reverend Jones remembered my name, I remembered my socks, he didn't ask for his book, and I didn't ask for my free carnation.

I returned his book the next day. As for the carnation, I had the grace to let it go.

Coyote Cools Out

(September 1991)

It is so hot humidity hangs in the air like a wet blanket heavy over a line. Human movement is limited to reaching for the telephone receiver to say "not home" to whomever calls. Going to work feels good because at least the place is air-conditioned.

You feel like a dog. You want to lie under the kitchen table and pant against the coolness of the kitchen floor.

In these dog days of summer, a lake is the Minnesota equivalent of the cool beneath the kitchen table. We locals hang out under the water with only the top of our heads exposed, raising our noses only to breathe.

My favorite urban lakes are Harriet and Cedar because they are spring-fed and stay the coolest, never totally mimicking the dog day air.

They are not the lakes of spring. Those are Calhoun and the other shallow ones that warm up swiftly, the ones where you can swim a few days after the ice goes out. But by the dog days, they are soup. Swimming through them becomes a struggle against the tentacles of milfoil and the grease of perspiration.

Any lake is better than no lake for a swim in the dog days, but only really cold water totally refreshes—exhilarates the spirit, tightens and smoothes the skin, polishes the mind, makes death seem inconsequential. To experience this priceless elixir my family takes an annual August trip to an island in the northern Great Lakes, reservoir to nearly one fifth of all the fresh surface water on planet Earth.

The Lake Huron region also sweltered, so when an acquaintance invited us on his boat for an evening cruise, we jumped aboard. A full moon illuminated the night and spread a swath of silver over water dark as wine.

The lake surface was glassy, but rollers from the previous day's storm rocked us until we anchored in the lee of a neighboring island.

An Indian friend on the boat knew this spot well. He had fished every bay in the region, rescued floundering swimmers, recovered corpses of the drowned. He knew not only the currents, temperatures and shorelines of the lake, but the contours of the bottom as well. So when he immediately vaulted over the side into the blackness, I jumped too, along with Mrs. Coyote and several others.

Yea though I dive into the water of the darkness of death, I fear no evil, for thou oh coolness art with me.

The cold water pulled my breath up short. I burst up from the black depths into a shower of white moonlight.

As we stroked through the lake's cold black silk, the shoreline glowed as moonlight illuminated the limestone pebbles. Dark cedar and spruce etched the rim of the sky. An abandoned lighthouse stood against the moon. We held bubbles of silken moonlight in our hands.

The dog days of summer have finally ended. The gong and clang of school and work ring out. The powerful flywheel of the real world is spinning again.

The children have new teachers to worry about, new school books to lose, old bicycles to be stolen, fresh leaves to rake.

Their parents refocus on house payments, repairing curbs and cleaning gutters, fixing parks, balancing state and federal budgets, building art centers and homeless shelters, all in the rhythm of a good day's work as the sense of impending winter drives us into a frenzy of usefulness. Everything that absolutely must be accomplished probably will be.

We attack these problems with zest because we have been renewed. Our skin, our lungs, our hearts remember—and look forward to again—the deep, cold water of midnight in the dog days of summer when we swam in coolness, our bodies awake and alive, our spirits drinking moonlight from a silver cup, our souls spread across a shimmering bay at the heart of one fifth of all the fresh surface water on planet Earth.

Why I Missed Palio

(October 1991)

Until now I have never missed Palio, the annual neighborhood festival. After all, Mrs. Coyote organized its predecessor over a decade ago, and we both believe fervently in celebrating the interconnectedness of urban community life. Last year was typical.

I got up early on Palio Sunday and ran off to Burch Pharmacy to buy crepe paper to decorate the Little One's bicycle. I dug out of the garage the old wagon I use to pull my stuffed Coyote in the parade, a wagon made just for this purpose by my handy neighbor Paul. The Little One and I decorated her bike too long and were late for the beginning of the parade, but joined up early enough to cruise by the reviewing stand and win a multiplicity (a neighborhood?) of awards: Best Parading Neighborhood Newspaper Columnist, Best Dressed Neighborhood Newspaper Columnist With Stuffed

Animal Logo, Best Decorated Bicycle next to the Worst Dressed Neighborhood Newspaper Columnist.

If the presence of the Urban Coyote is a virtual guarantee of glory in the neighborhood hall of fame, then how could he not attend this year? Coyote faced a cruel dilemma.

Over the summer the Littlest Coyote, now nine, developed an interest in the wonders of nature. Some of this new interest no doubt related to the fine instruction available to her at tiny Camp Lawton under the wise and careful tutelage of neighborhood park center Rats Paul, Van and Damon, who operate the camp located on a nearby weedy Wisconsin lake for a neighborhood Episcopal church. She survived the week quite excited, in spite of several midnight attacks by fellow campers covering unsuspecting sleepers with shaving cream while they slept, a quaint camp tradition. On the way home, she related wide-eyed how one afternoon Paul blew on a whistle, making a wounded rabbit sound, and a huge raptor flew into the camp meadow to investigate. She wasn't sure what kind of bird it was, but it *might* have been an eagle. That experience, and the shaving cream, more than made up for her inability to swim in the lake all week due to an outbreak of swimmer's itch.

Faced with her enthusiasm, I promised in June that I would take her to Hawk Watch Weekend in September at Hawk Ridge in Duluth. September is the month when hundreds of thousands of broad-winged hawks and other raptors make their way past the tip of Lake Superior on their annual migration from Canada to wintering grounds in Central and South America, a spectacular sight I had witnessed several times before.

I realized as well that the Littlest One had never been camping with her family before. Somehow over the years

Mr. and Mrs. Coyote had lost our joyful enthusiasm for the cold hard ground under a sleeping bag. But feeling fatherly and enthusiastic, I promised to camp out at Spirit Mountain with her that weekend as well. She could bring a friend.

I realized only much later that this selfless decision to cramp my body would end up cramping three other powerful urges as well. Born and raised near Green Bay, Wisconsin, I have no choice but to make fall football games part of the seasonal agony and ecstasy of my life. The second urge is church, which now feeds the life of my mind and spirit. The third is Palio, the annual celebration of the life of our community. Community is my religion, and I take my religion seriously.

Finally my promise to a nine-year-old had to take precedence. Does anyone disagree?

The Littlest One, her best friend Choulette and I departed for Duluth Saturday afternoon and arrived at Spirit Mountain in time to secure an exceptional camping spot in a maple glade next to a black granite boulder. The tent fit exquisitely on soft duff between two exposed roots. The firewood, mostly maple, was plentiful, I suspect because of the drought last year which left the maples with many dead branches in their crowns.

Before we built our fire and cooked dinner, we hiked along the ridge offering spectacular views of the St. Louis River valley and the harbors of Duluth, Minnesota and Superior, Wisconsin. Huge iron ore loading docks protruded into the estuary like dinosaur skeletons. We were thrilled to spot two Cooper's hawks in the trees at sunset resting for the next leg of their journey.

We ate like kings and queens. We roasted hot dogs over the fire until the skins split and blackened. We served them with pork and beans cooked inside the can nestled in the coals, garnished with fresh cut carrots, followed by marshmallows flambé on freshly trimmed sticks.

As the Littlest One worked to carefully put out the coals of the fire one by one, savoring each of them, she said she didn't want to leave this place. Ever. Or at least for a week.

Up on Hawk Ridge the next day the wind blew blustery and cold. The appointed day for the Vikings game and the Palio festival could not have been worse for hawks. With the wind blowing out of the south/southwest at 30 miles an hour or more, Lake Superior whipped into a froth below us. Through our binoculars we watched a huge taconite ore carrier struggle toward Duluth with waves crashing white halos over its bow. This is the kind of day sensible raptors stay in the trees waiting for more favorable conditions.

A glance at the official raptor count kept on Hawk Ridge by biologist Kim Eckert revealed far more favorable conditions the Wednesday before. On that day, 23,941 broad-winged hawks passed over the ridge, plus more than 400 sharp-shinned hawks and numerous red-tails, Cooper's, marsh hawks, kestrels, owls and eagles.

On our day, Sunday, September 22, 1991, eleven sharpies had been sighted from dawn to two in the afternoon. We saw one of them, struggling low against the wind, one-eleventh of the total daily tally.

Still, we had a wonderful time. Abandoning the ridge to the wind, we hiked well-marked trails down the backside into a cathedral of red pines that caused us to pause silently in its hush. On the way home, the girls scrambled like delighted monkeys around pools sculpted in red rock by the many waterfalls of the Sucker River as the sun broke through the clouds and warmed the day wrapped around us.

Driving home that night, I listened as the girls chattered with exhausted joy, then fell asleep.

As for the Vikings, they proved surprisingly easy to miss. The brief highlight videos on the 10:00 p.m. news of the 23-0 loss to New Orleans proved more than adequate.

As for Palio, I hope the neighborhood missed me as much as I missed it. However, eating like a king in the company of two princesses, three hawks and a hush of pines is a fine community too. And by all accounts I can gather, this year's celebration of urban neighborhood life and vitality succeeded remarkably well without the presence of one of its most ardent believers. That, of course, is how real community—and religion—works.

Yes, Minnesota, There Is a Santa Claus

(November 1991)

My nine-year-old has recently heard some unpleasant rumors. It seems some of her school friends have hinted that Santa Claus is a doubtful proposition.

When the subject of Santa came up at home recently, she smiled knowingly. "It's your parents," she said. We were shocked at this first public indication of heresy. We protested, but she was firm. "Nope, it's your parents," she said with folded arms, a wise smile, twinkling eyes. For a lightning bolt of evidentiary clarity, she added, "And anyway, I went and looked up the chimney. There is no way that anyone could get down there!"

We were saddened but not surprised by her skepticism. Our other children, all older, had developed a similar misunderstanding at about this age. We recalled our own years of apostasy from the truth.

But truth is truth, and it will win out. Santa Claus is as real as the ice and snow we are currently anticipating with absolute certainty despite little immediate evidence.

What is the evidence for Santa? Why, the persistence and necessity of the story, of course.

Supporting evidence immediately presented itself in our kitchen. The nine-year-old's nineteen-year-old brother happened to be a witness to her outburst of benighted certainty. He was appalled. He defended the magical nature of Santa Claus, that he can be a zillion places at once, that for such a guy coming down a chimney is as easy as picking his nose. These days he can come through heat ducts, radiator pipes, air conditioners! A chimney is the old and easy way. Didn't she remember hearing the reindeer on the roof? He did. What do school kids know anyway? They are ignorant bozos.

That she remained unconvinced is a testament to her immaturity plus the power of uninformed peer pressure. That he made such a spirited defense, unprompted, is one of the many proofs of the Santa story.

What does my son have to gain by perpetuating such a tale if it weren't true? And what would parents, those indicted by the sly young lady only minutes before, have to gain by perpetuating a falsehood to their children? Parents don't lie, they simply know all the facts.

They know that life is short, winter is long, and celebration is necessary. They know that life without compelling traditional stories is bereft of a huge dimension of continuity and community. They know that the occasions of gifting others, so selfish in youth, become selfless later on.

Here in Minnesota, in a climate where winter temperatures can approach absolute zero, a midwinter festival of gift giving approaches absolute truth. Unsurprisingly, Santa Claus is a northern tradition.

For another proof of the Santa story, imagine the negative. What would life be like in his absence?

Poor J. Alfred Prufrock, the alienated cynic in T. S. Eliot's poem of the same name: he measured out his life in coffee spoons. A full, rich life demands rituals far grander than coffee spoons. Otherwise living is reduced to the despairing details of parking tickets, senate hearings, neighborhood meetings, work and time off from work, school and vacations from school, and long dark winters in front of ignorant television sets.

Fortunately here comes Santa Claus, here comes Santa Claus right down the chimney of these problems. Santa's generous presence is essential to survival in the best of winters as well as the worst of winters.

Neither is the relentless exploitation of Santa Claus by the soulless engines of commerce a charge against the story. Instead, it's another proof of its validity. Santa can survive anything, including street corner impersonators wearing badly tailored Santa suits and cotton beards and wasted eyes. Even the youngest children see through these frauds immediately while maintaining a firm belief in the real thing.

Children's excited anticipation is the best proof of all. For them we put the seasonal candles on the mantle slowly, one at a time. Open only a single Advent calendar window a day, and don't peek! Make lists. Check them twice, thrice, mice. Let visions of sugarplums and Legos dance through their heads. With them we feel the slow stirring inside us of the ancient midwinter stories of birth and of gift-giving. We watch as every person in the community, many in spite of themselves, plays a necessary part in the powerful drama of a jolly old man winging his way across the heavens bearing burdens of joy just for you.

And if he doesn't come for you this year, what then? Then next year he will come—next year, next year, next year forever. For Santa is a true story, a midwinter promise bringing hope to all. We look forward to our daughter's rediscovery of him soon.

Murder in the Neighborhood

(December 1991)

A young woman is dead, assaulted, raped and murdered in her apartment in the heart of this neighborhood, only blocks from any of us.

The woman, 21, from Kansas, picked our neighborhood as the place to launch her adult life. She assured her parents that this particular city, and our particular neighborhood, were safe.

Yet someone broke into her basement apartment and was waiting when she got home.

Suspicion fell everywhere—on our friends who own the

duplex, on their brother who was visiting from Washington, DC, on neighbors.

Fortunately, the police soon caught the real culprit—a drifter from Texas with a long record of vicious assaults, sexual and otherwise. His DNA matched. He had wandered up our neighborhood streets at random, sort of blown in. He could have landed in any neighborhood, on any street, in any house with an unlocked back door. But it was this one.

We've had our fair share of after-midnight human visitors. The ones that break car windows and rip off radios. That break basement windows and rip off televisions. That enter unlocked back doors and rip off purses while you sleep in the next room. They drive us crazy.

Now we have a new kind. A rapist. A murderer. He killed more than a young woman, which is way beyond horror enough. He put a spike through the heart of our community.

So now your wife or daughter wants to walk the dog? Forget it. They want to walk to the store at night? Forget it. Want to dance in the street under the streetlight to celebrate a winter snowfall? Forget it. Want to come home and feel safe alone? Forget it.

Because someone may be lurking in the dark. Some vicious predator may be lurking in the dark.

Safety is an intangible. You have it or you don't. In general, we have had it and fear does not rule us.

Now our perception of safety has altered. Until this predator is tried, convicted and put away forever, safety will remain a concern.

You will hear a lot in the coming weeks about locking doors and windows at home at all times, joining block clubs and other means to protect one another. All of this must be done.

Men particularly must participate. Not only are we less vulnerable to this kind of predator, but our honor as males is at stake. Sexual predators steal the dignity from every one of us.

My wife, the ferocious Mrs. Coyote, is going one step further. She is getting organized.

She is starting a group called WATCH, "We're at the Court House." Her goal is to create an energized and persistent cadre of volunteers to monitor sexual violence trials to make sure guilty predators like this drifter don't continue to go free; to lobby legislators to enact strict sentencing practices for repeat sexual offenders; to educate children and the public on issues of violence; to research methods to counteract same; and to build public campaigns against media exploitation of same. She's in it for the long haul.

I predict this group will have an enormous constituency. The Urban Coyote is joining. Are you?

Some may say such measures are unrealistic. That we ought to get used to the occasional rape and murder, the way we've had to get used to bicycle thefts, car break-ins, household thefts. This is modern times, they say. Violent craziness is just a part of big city living. Nothing serious going on here at all compared to, say, St. Louis, Detroit or the Bronx. Minnesotans in general, and this neighborhood's residents in particular, have it good. Think of those kids and parents in the Bronx with gunfire outside the door every night. Now *they* have it tough.

Yes they do. Things have gotten way out of hand in the Bronx. It's not going to happen here. We are stopping it now.

Today sadness and fear stalk the neighborhood. As we look over our shoulders and inside ourselves we must vow that we will never forget this young woman, that parents around the world are right to trust that their children have a safe future in our homes and our neighborhood.

Slouching Towards Television to Be Bored

(May 1992)

Recent studies have noted that watching television reduces one's metabolism, heart rate, blood sugar, brain waves, SAT scores and conversational ability, while increasing butt sores, carbohydrate poisoning (potato chip variety) and family anxiety.

None of this comes as a surprise to Mrs. Coyote. She has seen me walk near a television set. I slow down. My jaw drops to my chest. My frame softens into a slouch. My feet root to the floor. I am impervious to conversation. When the television set is actually turned on, I am even worse.

Numerous informal studies by Mrs. C. confirm that whatever content the cathode rays project is irrelevant—soap operas, commercials for diet drinks, shows embodying clean family values (were there any), shows involving violence and sex (were there any without), beefy football contests—no matter, the slouch is the same. The medium is the message—I watch, therefore I slouch.

Mrs. C. finds this addiction more than a little disturbing, particularly since, under similar circumstances, she suffers no such ill effects.

I deal with this problem by physically avoiding television sets as much as possible before they can reach out and grab me. In addition, I would be willing to attend "Tubaholics Anonymous" meetings were there any, where I would be forced to face the horror of admitting in public that I twice watched *Knott's Landing*.

In spite of my slouch, the Coyotes have raised a litter of fine children, measured by most standards of literacy and decency. They all read and love books, brush their teeth and do not actively shame their elders in public. We have accomplished this feat with a variety of careful rules about television usage evolved over twenty-five years of parenthood.

Here, then, is the Urban Coyote Sloucher's Guide to Television Wisdom.

Initially, we owned no television set at all. Our first three children spent their preschool years tube-free. Finally, however, a television set crept in. Well, the truth is, I carried it in. A lifelong Green Bay Packers fan, I felt I could no longer live a full life without the ritual of fall football so important in my childhood.

Mrs. C. was disgusted, and her reaction proved justified. The evil box took over the house. Soon Saturday morning cartoons and the evening news became household staples along with my Sunday afternoon football fixes.

Good fortune shone upon us two years later. Our babysitter accidentally knocked the set off its temporary perch atop the stove and it shattered. She was mortified when we returned home, but we just grinned and paid her a bonus. The wicked witch was dead! We were free!

Unfortunately, my football addiction compelled me to tiptoe back in with another TV several years later. By that time, however, three young children were well on their way to becoming human beings as opposed to tube-sucking androids. They were reading and enjoying it.

The TV took over the house again, of course. But we were strong enough to maintain reasonable rules for many years, such as no TV during the school week. Even so, the set found itself with increasing frequency on the kitchen counter, no longer treated like an escaped felon but more like a valued kitchen appliance.

Now the first three children are grown and out of the house. Only the Littlest Coyote—ten years old and ten years younger than the youngest above her—remains a concern. Imagine, therefore, our joy when she came to her father one day with this request: Would it be OK if she did not watch TV for a year? I was elated but suspicious. Voluntarily give up the opiate of the masses?

Why, I asked. Simple, she answered. She and her big sister had decided to buy a horse ranch in Montana so she needed to begin saving money immediately. If she stopped watching TV for a year, I had to fork over $100 to her savings account.

Ahh, the old ranch-in-Montana fantasy! The girls schemed that they would live out their lives in the mountains, just the two of them, with a corral of Ol' Paints, far from the madding crowd in general and boys in particular. I closed my eyes and imagined myself riding Ol' Paint through the Big Horn Mountains, sagebrush under my feet, the huge blue sky overhead filled with soaring . . . buzzards eager to pick my broken bones.

OK, so I'm no horseman. Still, a Montana ranch fantasy has the power to compel useful Minnesota behavior. I agreed to the deal immediately, suspecting that no one—certainly no child carrying my genes—could refrain from television watching for a full year.

She did it. During that year, she read a lot of books, sold Girl Scout cookies and rented a lot of weekend movies with her baby-sitter (a loophole). She watched TV at home only with the rare sanction of her parents (let's face it, winter Olympic ice skating and the fall World Series were essential for spiritual bonding with the larger community).

The year is up. I'm paying, gladly.

The Montana ranch fantasy encouraged local imagination, education, thrift, persistence and self-discipline. Beats the heck out of what I learned watching, slack-jawed, *Knott's Landing* the other night.

Maybe we'll get lucky and another baby-sitter or visiting friend will knock our tube off the kitchen counter and break it. Then, however briefly, our family stories and fantasies will again be fully our own.

What I Did on
My Summer Vacation

(September 1992)

On my vacation this summer I wrote a poem. It went like this.

On August 22nd my son, the Big Guy, was married. For the wedding, all six Coyote family members played unfamiliar roles: junior bridesmaid, bridesmaid, best man, mother of the groom, father of the groom, and of course

groomed groom. I am happy to report that we all performed adequately.

The groom's ponytail was neatly tied back throughout the
service and his rented tuxedo straddled his 6' 4" frame handsomely. This regal outfit was set off nicely by black shoes with
worn-out heels and sagging white socks. Nobody would have
noticed these two homey details but for the extensive kneel-
ing the service required, exposing the gleaming worn hobnails. His father was warmed by the familiar touch.

Mrs. Coyote worked like a dog to make sure that beauty,
joy and clockwork were the hallmarks of the occasion. I was
in charge of supplying the booze and transportation, and
arranged that all would be well served.

My problem arose two days before the wedding day. The
bride and groom asked me to read something at the service.
Even by my lax organizational standards, this was a bit of
short notice. I demurred but they said that members of the
bride's family had agreed to read. In the spirit of balance,
I assented.

I had two manuscripts of poetry with me—one written by
a friend, the other by me. Fortunately I quickly found appropriate, and appropriately short, poems in both. From my
friend Richard O. Moore's unpublished manuscript, *Over
Time*, I selected "The Wedding", which included these wonderful lines:

> *It is a most intricate web.*
> *There are animals who die*
> *From the shock of it.*

The priest, a canny veteran of hundreds of weddings and
marriage counseling sessions, later told me he burst into joyful laughter when he heard those lines.

From my own manuscript, a twenty-six-year work in progress called *A Marriage Book*, I selected "Marriage"—a sententious editorial built on a physical metaphor:

> *It is gravity,*
> *which limits us totally,*
> *which makes all things possible.*

I was set.

The morning of the wedding I awoke earlier than usual, the dog whimpering at my hand. He wanted breakfast and a walk. I made coffee in the silent kitchen and walked him on our familiar route into the woods. We went farther than usual and found a raspberry patch full of small, late season berries. I picked a handful and carried them home in my empty cup for Mrs. Coyote's breakfast. In the silence of early morning light, I sat down at the kitchen table and, to my surprise, began to write.

For the first time in all the months of intense wedding planning, the power and emotion of the day broke through me. A vein opened to the center of the earth and spilled onto my notebook. As I wrote, I cried. A friend arriving early to help set up the house, turned quietly away when he saw me.

I knew this was the poem I had to read at the wedding that afternoon.

Mrs. Coyote and I rode in the last carriage leaving for the church. She was regal, aware and proudly in control. As we rode off to the church, she signaled a friend to close an upstairs shutter that had blown open, fixing the last detail.

I was huffing like a stevedore. I was trying to calm myself to deliver the poem that had washed over me that morning. How could I recite it without choking up?

Throughout our arrival at the church, our formal entrance

and seating in the front pew and the unloading of wads of toilet paper Mrs. C. had wisely stuffed into my pockets, I was breathing like a sprinter pumping up for the starting line.

Through the emergence of the groomed groom and his handsome best man (so that's what our second son looks like without his baseball hat on backwards), the magnificent procession of the flowered bridesmaids and dignified groomsmen, the glory of our breathtaking eldest daughter in the procession, the strength of our youngest daughter as she held the hand of the flower girl, the triumphant glacial flow of the stunning bride, I measured each breath. Hold, release. Hold, release.

As the bride and groom kneeled, she a sculpture of white, he with ponytail and hobnails shining, the priest called up the first reader. Then he called on me. I breathed one last time.

Following is the poem I recited at our son's wedding, when the celebration of the commitment of two young people to each other turned the details of our family life into something much greater than the sum of all planning and anxiety and hope.

THE MORNING OF THE WEDDING
(for Jamie and Laurie)

On our early morning walk, the dog, unwell, eats grass.
A tug labors a barge toward a splash of sunlight
on the horizon.
Four cormorants fly by my shoulder.
Gulls carry on their obnoxious calling.

August 22, 1992. August?
No more than any other month.

Yet in the peace of early morning light
among the small ripe raspberries
of this late summer season,
with the clap of horses rising the hill,
the world is changed forever
by these two courageous children.

As they kneel and touch an old gold ring
and make it burst into flame before us
with a few quiet syllables
from their bursting hearts,
mathematics and grammar implode:
two becomes one,
I do becomes we are,
and infinity, that shimmering abstraction,
twists together into a particular double helix.

The splash of sunlight on the lake
winked at me three times.

The coffee this morning,
smoothed with milk,
flavored with raspberries,
is better than usual.

Now that I think of it, I have been holding my breath in odd
and unusual ways ever since the birth of this first child nearly
twenty-six years ago. As I stepped down from the podium, I
breathed easily, as if I were born again.

PART FOUR

A HIGH AND HOLY CALLING

1993-94

Rising Up With the WESAC Flames

(May 1993)

Last summer our oldest daughter, aged twenty-three, met some powerful women in the campaign of young Bill Clinton, soon to become President of the United States. She was deeply impressed by their working at such responsible jobs in such an important enterprise. She asked one of them what gave her the confidence as a woman to play in the big leagues with the big boys. "Team sports," the woman answered unequivocally.

Next thing I knew, the eldest daughter ordered our youngest daughter, age eleven, to sign up for the upcoming basketball season operated by the city park system. Great, I said. It will be fun to watch the games.

The sign-up form our daughter brought home asked parents to check a box describing their own level of participation. Coach? Assist? Drive to games? I hesitated, wary as a coyote sniffing a piece of fresh venison laid suspiciously in the middle of the trail. Definitely a trap. All parents who value their time never mark any of those boxes.

That I marked the "assist" box is an indication of my failing memory, for I had played this game before.

Fifteen years earlier, when our first three children were young, the eldest wanted to play basketball. Problem was, there were no organized youth teams in the neighborhood.

The previous volunteer basketball czar had retired once his son moved on to high school. No one picked up his crown. Then I came along.

I called him to find out what I could do. The next thing I knew I was the commissioner of youth basketball in the west area of the city, the West Side Athletic Club, or WESAC.

In those days there was no Kenwood Park Center, no helpful park board staff, no help at all. I typed up and printed the application forms, distributed them to the four area schools, gathered fees from the parents, ordered t-shirts with numerals on the back, purchased balls and scheduled practice times at various school gymnasiums in the area all operated by janitor-tyrants.

And I had to recruit coaches. I used every trick, starting with innocent-seeming questions on the application form, ending with the empty threat that a child couldn't play unless her parent agreed to coach.

My basketball hegemony lasted throughout the junior high basketball careers of our two sons, at which point I happily passed the czar's crown to the capable head of neighbor Cal Hanson, whose basketball-playing son had returned home after college and wanted to coach.

I had paid my dues. No more late night pleading with janitors for gym time. No more trips to sport shops to pick up t-shirts and shorts in the wrong sizes. No more wheedling naive parents into coaching for their children's teams. I was free!

So I knew better than to check any box for my daughter. I was hardly surprised, therefore, when the current WESAC basketball czar called me up.

"Coyote," he said, "here's the deal. Five girls have signed up: two ten-year olds, two twelves, one eleven. If you can figure out how to make a team out of this group, you can coach it." "Why me?" I asked, knowing the answer. "No other parent marked any of the boxes," he responded.

"By the way," he added, "I talked to your daughter on the phone yesterday. She named the team the WESAC Flames. I already sent it in to park board headquarters."

He was way too tricky. I was doomed.

I called the five girls and told them to immediately recruit more school friends to fill out the team. I called the park center to reserve practice time. Both strategies were successful. Sort of.

Seventeen girls signed up, far too many. Worse, they came from three different age categories, hence different basketball divisions, but not enough to make a solid team in any two of them. This meant we had to play in the eleven-and-twelve-year-old division, but with a majority of players younger than that. Trouble.

Worse, the only practice time I could wrangle from the heavily booked Park Center was Sunday noon, and that was due to the generosity of the center director who agreed to personally open up the gym for my team as the center was normally closed on Sunday.

That meant I would have to curtail all my revered Sunday morning rituals—reading two Sunday newspapers, attending church, seeking out peace and quiet—for three months! I took it.

After a few practices, it soon became evident that the WESAC Flames suffered from another serious problem. Me. Even though I play basketball regularly and once organized the regional teams, I had no clue how to coach. With the telephone advice of several parents and two new books on coaching, I desperately studied coaching techniques. This education proved too late to help the team.

But the seventeen girls astonished me. A duchess's mixture of ages, basketball interests and talents, they were energetic, interested, individualistic and respectful of the coach. They were an honor to get to know, as were their families.

Coaching a child's sport, even when you don't have the time and don't know how, is a commitment that repays itself many time over in community well being. In the process of calling players, you get to know their parents. They respect the gift of time you give to their daughters. You respect the gift of their daughter. The result of this mutual admiration society is a widening and strengthening of the web of community.

As for the games, we lost to the two best teams in the league, well practiced, expertly coached and with players as tall as redwoods, by about fifty points each. We were more competitive against the other teams but lost by double digits as well. But in our penultimate game, we put it all together. Play Number 1 worked, as did play Number 2. So did the out-of-bounds play. Our shots fell. Our rebounders rebounded. Our guards guarded. Our forwards forwarded. We won twenty-one to seventeen.

The players cheered and romped. Their parents stood and cheered. And the reluctant coach, his thumbed over basketball books at his side, did his best not to show his pride. He failed. He rose up and cheered with the WESAC Flames.

How I Write Poetry

(August 1993)

When I go on vacation I invariably bring along some important project that I can't find time to finish during the normal work season.

Sometimes I actually work on the project. More often I work on nothing at all, which is what my body and mind know I am supposed to be doing while on vacation. Sometimes, however, if I am lucky, I write a poem. It goes like this.

I sit down at my keyboard to begin the overdue project. But my relaxed mind is tuned to a deeper, wider current. I reach into it first with my hands and feel it flow over and around the pebbles of my fingertips.

At such moments, I try to capture those currents in poetry. I used to do this very late at night, after work and dinner, with babies asleep and only the owls out patrolling. Then the poetry might squeeze its way under the doorway like mice. If lucky, I would find small, smooth bones lying on the typewriter in the morning.

After the children crossed the teenage threshold and began staying up later at night than I could, early morning became the poetry time, the undisturbed hour after sunrise when the family still slept and the robins were out catching worms and the kestrels were out catching robins. If lucky, I would sometimes find a small blue egg or a tuft of orange feathers nested on my typewriter before I left for work.

During this year's vacation at our cottage on Mackinac Island, I planned to write a long meditative essay compiling the lessons I learned from twenty years of teaching American Indian Literature. I had even lined up an obliging magazine editor to give the piece the weight of a deadline.

But first, why not catch up on a few novels? Vacation is one of the few times I can read novels, unless required by my reading group, reflecting a sad lack of personal reading discipline. So the first thing I did this vacation was read three sequential novels by Barbara Kingsolver. That rich experience, plus biking with the kids, running over the electric cord with the electric lawn mower, picking berries, grilling fish, drinking with relatives and watching birds, consumed most of my ten vacation days. As I finished the last novel, *Animal Dreams*, tears of emotion ran down my cheeks.

Early the next morning, after making coffee and walking the dog, I chased an elusive pileated woodpecker through the woods with binoculars. Back at the kitchen table, I wrote to family and co-workers on postcards picturing local Indian chiefs. Then I entered the back bedroom to begin the essay project.

The back room of the cottage holds an old bureau, a rickety wooden chair and a table next to the window that looks out into thick cedar woods. I love this place, silent as a monastery. The flat green fingertips of the cedars ensnare all sound, even breeze, as does the soft brown cedar duff carpeting the ground.

I opened my grocery bag full of accumulated research and spread the contents around me on the floor. I happened upon a book I'd forgotten I'd brought with me, my much worn copy of *Cold Mountain* poems by Han-shan.

Han-shan! Brother!

Twenty-two years ago I came upon Han-shan's one hundred *Cold Mountain* poems translated by Burton Watson. A friend gave me the book just prior to a long retreat with fellow staff members from the school where I worked. As we drove in the van I read the poems out loud. We all laughed until we were weak. Han-shan's personal laments, witty observations and broad insights, all in accessible conversational speech, sounded as familiar to me as if written by an older brother. Yet Han-shan lived, if he lived at all and isn't a literary fiction, more than a thousand years ago on the coast of China. Once a family man and government worker, he spent the end of his life a hermit meditating and laughing out loud on the wild slopes of Cold Mountain, inscribing his few poems on rocks and trees.

As the school car rolled on in silence, I began to write my own responses to Han-shan's voice. Twenty years later I am still writing to him.

I put down the essay and read number 39.

> *The birds and their chatter overwhelm me with feeling:*
> *At times like this I lie down in my straw hut.*
> *Cherries shine with crimson fire.*
> *Willows trail slender boughs.*
> *The morning sun pops from the jaws of blue peaks;*
> *Bright clouds are washed in the green pond.*
> *Who ever thought I would leave the dusty world*
> *and come bounding up the southern slope of Cold*
>   *Mountain?*

As I finished reading, the pileated woodpecker I had chased that morning landed on a birch right next to my window. As he worked around that fat trunk alone among the cedars, I watched in a hush. When he flew away, I wrote the following poem from the slope of my own Cold Mountain.

When sound leaks from a cedar grove, better listen!
A spiked shadow dances round a branch.
Then a woodpecker big as a hatchet taps out
his elusive forest story right in front of me!
I lean back breathless from my desk,
forgetting for a moment the chair is broken.
Who would have thought there'd be a place so quiet
that what is longed for comes right in?

So that's what I'd been seeking all week, a time quiet enough for feelings to flow, a space open enough for what arrives. That is the moment when poets write not what comes to our minds but what comes out our fingers through pencils or typewriters or laptop computers, a direct connection to the soul through touch.

No one need verify such moments of the unlocked spirit. What arrives may fly away in an instant. Or remain fresh for a thousand years.

Coyote Learns to Dance

(October 1993)

Mrs. Johnson's dancing school in her linoleum-floored basement in DePere, Wisconsin was not an environment conducive to learning to dance. Not only was the room cold, poorly lit by the small, high windows and crowded by the arms of the old coal furnace, but girls were there, classmates from my elementary school down the street.

As a fifth grade boy, I was still quite wary of girls, especially in the matter of getting close to them. So when Mrs. Johnson made me pair up with tall Sharon or round Jane or winsome Elizabeth, this violation of my natural repulsion caused an apparent deformation of my memory related to the activity at hand. The repulsion from girls fortunately proved temporary, but the problem with dancing has proven permanent. I simply can't learn the correct steps.

Not that I haven't danced since fifth grade. Chubby Checker's twist freed me in high school to dance without thinking. Since then I've become a whirling dervish on the dance floor—swinging my partner under this arm and that, up and back and round and round, throwing in some Indian toe steps and African jump squats, Western two steps and dance hall knee kicks, monkey pumps and twisting towel-offs, ending by cradling her in a deep back-bending dip that leaves us both exhausted with pleasure.

To my knowledge, only one woman has required extended hospitalization after these endeavors. Her arm somehow came out of her socket at the shoulder.

Minor injuries have been more numerous—blackened toes, torn toenails, flattened arches, sprained ankles, bruised calves, scuffed shoes of all descriptions, these have afflicted not only my various partners but random other dancers within the range of my activities on the floor.

Mrs. Coyote has not been a stoic throughout these whirling enthusiasms. Dancing with me makes her crazy.

My uncontrolled zest is only one of her problems. She likes to lead, or at least to lead me.

She has good reason to want to take control. Not only am I somewhat without dance training, she is a trained dancer. She feels a pedagogical desire to help me straighten out and dance right.

Problem is I too expect to lead. I remember that much from Mrs. Johnson's dancing class: guys lead, girls follow.

That approach works reasonably well with most other women, who seem to accept the attendant risks of dancing with me. However, it does not go down well with Mrs. Coyote.

In our twenty-seven years of marriage, some of our biggest fights have occurred after attempting to dance together. On numerous occasions she wanted to kill me. At least twice she tried.

After the last nearly fatal dance encounter, we came to an obvious conclusion—either terminate the marriage or take dancing lessons. After extended debate, we opted to try dancing lessons.

That was four years ago. Somehow the daily dance of life never seemed to allow us space on the dance school floor. During that period, we continued to endure occasional close encounters of the dance kind, with the usual disastrous results, except when Mrs. Coyote sensibly refused to dance with me at all, thus freeing us both to cut our separate swaths across the floor.

Then some friends asked us to join them for an evening of ballroom dancing. Knowing our weakness in this area, we demurred, but they persisted. Just come and watch, they said. The occasion was the Northern Lights Ballroom Dancing Championship.

By this time we had seen the quirky Australian film *Strictly Ballroom* about a young couple striving for first place in the Pan-Pacific ballroom dance competition. We thought the film was an outrageous and funny parody. Our friends said it was an accurate depiction of ballroom dance life. We were intrigued.

We would go and watch like anthropologists. We'd be entertained like moviegoers. We just wouldn't dance.

The date was set.

Then our friends slyly suggested that we'd have a much better time at the competition if we knew at least a few dance steps, so they had arranged introductory lessons for us. Wednesday, 6 p.m. Don't be late.

Mrs. Coyote panicked as we drove up to the Fred Astaire Dance Studio and she saw other couples through the storefront window. She is a private woman, and this clearly was not a private lesson. In addition, she knew her husband required a lot of work before anyone should be able to view him publicly.

I, on the other hand, felt a tingle of excitement. I like meeting new people. God knows I needed dance lessons. And I was still laughing over the Pan-Pacific.

Scott introduced himself, a slim youngish man with black pants, silk shirt and blond, slicked-back hair. A man on the move, with two jobs and a car phone, he was to be Susan's teacher. Cindy approached me. She had a lithe body with long, strong legs and brunette hair wrapped a French twist. She smiled. Where you from? I asked. I grew up in a small town in Wisconsin, she answered. So did I, I said. We hit it off right away, swapping stories of beer and cheddar cheese and Frank Lloyd Wright.

In the process of talking and dancing, I caught on.

I mastered the fox trot and the swing step—two dances basic to keeping feet away from other feet and men and women in harmony. Left, right, side-together, left, right, side-together. Side, side, rock-step, side, side, rock-step. I also learned how to hold a woman properly—right elbow wide, right hand on her shoulder blade, left elbow down, hand facing forward, maintaining an even space between. So *that's* how it's supposed to be done!

At the end of our one-hour lesson, Scott and Cindy brought Mrs. Coyote and me together for the last dance. A dangerous electricity crackled between us. Mrs. Coyote bit her lip. I feared for my life. Our instructors pulled us together, again going over the details—how to grasp hands, how to hold, how to lead, how to read.

Then, to the music of a slow fox trot, we stepped out across the floor. I stepped toward her with my left foot. She stepped back with her right. At the corners, we swung together. As we moved, we smiled.

Coyote Walks the Dog

(December 1993)

Every morning at 6:00 a.m., give or take a few minutes depending upon his digestion, the family dog licks my hand.

I have learned to be pleased by this reliable reinforcement of my clock radio. The concerned voices of National Public Radio too easily weave their stories into my dreams. Rufus the Wonder Dog reminds me that I am not actually standing on the wintry battlements of Sarajevo taunting Serbian aggressors while wearing nothing but socks. Rather, it is time to get up and begin morning rituals.

He seems satisfied, if not enthusiastic, about his handful of compressed grain nodules and bowl of fresh water. However, the prospect of a morning walk sends him bouncing with zest. Our block is his daily newspaper which he reads at every tree, bush and hydrant, plus the bathroom facilities in which to read it.

I am somewhat less zestful. After all, it is the cusp of winter sunrise, the sidewalks are icy and unshoveled, I am groggy, and his morning walk interrupts my own rituals of drinking fresh-perked coffee and reading the newspaper before members of the family interrupt me.

Still, since I'm the one who gets up earliest, I'm the one who walks the dog, even if he belongs to my daughter and is moderately small and shaggy white, hardly a proper mastiff to accompany an adult male through the streets of the 'hood.

Mrs. Coyote and our eldest daughter brought him home three years ago. I was shocked. My wife comes from an anti-dog family, the kind that shoots at the neighbor's barking hounds with BB guns. But as this daughter struggled with mood swings as a teenager and the puppy leaped into her arms at the pet store to console her, Mrs. C's heart melted and my dog-walking days began.

Therefore, today after feeding him and making coffee, I allowed his leaping enthusiasms to usher me slowly out the front door. On the porch, I removed the plastic bag from the newspaper, put the bag in my pocket, turned out the porch light and stepped toward the morning.

In the quiet of this early winter day, all the leaves had finally fallen from the boulevard trees. The graceful arms of the remaining American elms floated like black vines against the gray glowing sky. A male cardinal whistled five liquid notes.

In this urban neighborhood silence stirs all around me. On summer evenings I count the rasps of cicadas searching for lovers. In fall the lonely call of a gull floats over houses. In spring ice drips from eaves. In deep winter sparrows fluff up inside a protective buckthorn thicket.

Sometimes neighbor Paul Miller, an early riser, is at work in his front porch office, his face lit by the glow of the desk lamp. If we see each other, we wave. Occasionally neighbor Mike Reed emerges from his front door in his pajamas, or his wife Jane Tilka in her flowing nightgown, to retrieve the morning newspaper. If I am later than usual, several clumps of children huddle on corners waiting for school buses.

But most human encounters are with fellow dog walkers.

I know several people in the neighborhood better by their dogs' names than their own.

A new neighbor moved in across the street with Max, big as a bull. He looks like a wolf-husky cross with Babe the Blue Ox genes.

Cliff is a giant part-terrier mutt. Terriers are famous for their exuberance, and Cliff is no exception. When he first saw Rufus one morning, he bounded toward him from half a block away. Rufus appeared delighted by the prospect until Cliff bombed into him at full speed like a truck out of control, sending Rufus spinning like a car hit on the freeway. Cliff is as playful as Tigger in *Winnie the Pooh*. I love that dog.

After encountering Cliff many mornings and some evenings for over a year, I finally climbed out of my reverie long enough to seek the name of Clifford's owner. I forgot it immediately. But I can tell you he is a witty guy, has a new baby, is one of the first on the block to snowblow his walks and is a helluva dog owner. Since that first explosive encounter he has effectively taught the mighty Cliff to sit, stay and generally cease to Tigger-tumble fellow creatures. I miss Cliff's exuberance, although I am sure his family doesn't. Rufus the Wonder Dog learned to take evasive action. They have become friends, marking each other's scents with pinpoint accuracy.

Same with the springer spaniel that comes by on a long loop from the park early every morning. Leashless like Rufus, the spaniel stays well at the heels of a brisk-paced young man. The Rufus-spaniel encounter is marked by spaniel whines of affection until his owner gets 20 feet away, at which point the spaniel bolts back to him as if he were attached by a bungee cord.

This morning as Rufus and I rounded the block's icy back stretch, a neighbor emerged from her front door across the street. In a thick coat, her head wrapped in a scarf, she slowly worked her way down the front steps, making liberal use of the railing against the slipperiness. Once on the sidewalk she poked at the ice with her cane.

A not-well-trained Rufus ambled across the street to greet her leg.

As I walked over to retrieve him, she asked if I would help her down the icy driveway to her car. I offered her my arm. As she leaned on me she said how much she and her friends enjoy seeing the "puppy" on his walks around the block every morning, his friskiness and bounce. I didn't know she had been watching us.

I asked her if she was going to work this Friday after Thanksgiving, normally a holiday. She said yes, she's a typesetter. I said that clients seem to want her kind of projects faster than yesterday, which she agreed is par for her kind of business.

Once in her car, she thanked me and Rufus for our help,

again admiring his cheerfulness, then drove off toward her day at the keyboard, while I admired her cheerfulness in her wake.

Rufus and I rounded the block and headed home to this keyboard to pass on the neighborhood news gathered on our morning walk together. We paused only once more. I picked it up in a plastic bag and placed it in the garbage container.

A Solstice Call

(January 1994)

Every parent expects such a call sooner or later.

Ours came near midnight on a December night without snow.

The accident was horrendous. Their car skidded on black ice in the mountains of New Mexico and rolled down the mountain, finally stopped by a tree. The crushed car was wrapped around his wife like a cocoon. Our son fought his way out and climbed back up the mountain to the road for help.

When his voice reached us hours later, adrenaline crackled on the line. They were rescued. The cuts, the glass, the climb through the snow in stocking feet and bare hands were nothing. His neck is broken, but not too bad.

And she?

They were married a year ago last summer. We did not

know until this moment that the terrors as well as the joys of family are so treacherously extended by such a bond.

And she? He found it hard to talk. Her condition is less clear.

After a long night in which my wife and I stared at lights swirling around the room, each one a telephone, each phone ringing—after such a night the real morning phone call was reassuring. No brain damage. Little apparent spinal damage. Our son thought they both would go home—wearing collars—in a few days. Situation stable.

Our family's annual celebration of the winter solstice was scheduled for the next night. Traditionally it's a time when we celebrate with neighbors the turn of the year away from darkness toward the light. It is also an event at which we initiate our children into adulthood. When they turn twenty-one, they and their friends join us at the party as equals. This son was the first, initiated five years ago, now married with his own life in New Mexico.

Can we continue with the event? What to do or say? We decided we would tell the story. The guests are family, friends and neighbors of many years. They would understand.

At the party, we distributed notes describing the state of family affairs: the accident, the rescue, the apparently stable condition, the good long-term prognosis, the early Christmas present of their survival. My wife urged that the traditional messages of hope burned in the solstice fire be sent to all who are hurt, to all who must heal.

Once we broke the ice, similar stories flowed that night and throughout the following days.

One neighborhood friend described the frozen moment two years ago he received his call. A slightly nasal voice on the other end of the line identified himself as an administrator at his daughter's college. He then described the accident, the slow straightening of the line of her brain waves. My friend remembers with ferocious clarity that official voice, the sudden weight of the phone, the panic and emptiness.

Others told of stunning near misses. My sister recalled skidding off mountain roads twice, miraculously saved both times. Hearing the phrase, "black ice," her daughter told a story even her mother hadn't heard. About the time she hit black ice, lost control, and nearly plummeted off a deep ravine. Friends in the next car were preparing to call 911, certain she was going over.

My own experience includes a terrifying near miss nearly thirty years ago. Driving across the country with a college friend, my car spun out of control on a rain-flooded Nebraska highway. He would have been killed had we struck the telephone pole two feet further forward. Instead, at college reunions we laugh and exchange news about our jobs and families. We both remember that suspended moment with crystal clarity.

My sister's and niece's tangles with mountain roads and black ice—and mine with a telephone pole—proved to be of no consequence in our lives, except as frightening stories to tell or hide. For others, the call is irreversible. For others, a wait.

The call the day after the party held much scarier news. Both broken necks were much worse than supposed. They were being evaluated for spinal fusion operations. I flew down the next day, the family two days later.

By then our son's neck was stabilized in an external contraption called a "halo" he would have to wear for at least three months. It is awkward—four pins drilled into the surface of his skull attached to rods keeping his neck rigid—but his sense of humor is already working with the possibilities.

On Christmas Eve, our daughter-in-law underwent surgery to fuse two fractured vertebrae.

As we waited for the results of the surgery, and through the days of recovery, we grew to know other families playing out similar stories. The Salazar family hoped that their twenty-three-year-old son would wake up after a car accident the same night as our son's crash. They cheered the slightest evidence of responsiveness, and we with them. The Garcia family awaited word of their children's recovery also from two broken necks in a car crash. "Merry Christmas," Joe Garcia said to me on Christmas Eve. "Things gotta get better."

In the season of the New Year, we are more cognizant than ever of the fulcrum of hope and fear. The near misses and the crushing blows. The extended joys of children, family and community, and the extended risks.

Sharing the risks, testing the bonds built by blood and commitment and time together, yields the confidence to tell the stories.

Our children, extricated from a car crushed around them, should recover. Others wait for any sign of hope—in emergency rooms around the country, and in the world's neighborhoods, villages, barrios. At this turning point of the northern winter season, the increase in light is imperceptible. For some, darkness still looms.

May our experience prove for many that the darkness will not hold. That the light can and will return.

Winter Escapes

(January 1994)

January 1994 contained bipolar swings in temperature and mood. The month opened with temperatures thirty below zero Fahrenheit plus an incalculable wind chill that stilled car batteries, froze household pipes, buried farmhouses, inconvenienced many and depressed everybody. At the same time, the Governor's decision to close schools throughout the state elicited yelps of ecstasy from 800,000 public school students. Even if hopes for a second day off did not materialize, the kids' release from a pressurized school day probably contributed to the rapid warming we have since seen blossom around us.

When the Littlest Coyote, a silver-braced sixth grader, heard the school closing announcement over the radio, she pulled her fist toward her chest with a whistling "Yesssss!!!"

Remember that feeling? I sure do.

My high school, a boarding school, was an academic grind—study, study, day and night. Late in the semester, the pressure built so high a psychological snap was in the air. Every student frantically swam upstream. Papers or projects were due with no time left to do them. The place was ready to blow.

School officials must have understood, for they had developed a clever tradition to deal with it. Each semester included a secret day off, sort of a planned surprise. Every student and teacher knew the day was coming, but none knew exactly when, teachers included.

As pressure built throughout the semester, students madly speculated that the magic free day had to be tomorrow or certainly the day after. Only a day off could save us from being crushed by the impossible deadlines cresting over us.

One morning, when we could stand it no longer, the special bell finally rang just before breakfast! Everyone cheered madly. Racked bodies and spirits miraculously straightened. No classes! Yessss!!!

Everyone, teachers and students alike, spent the first part of the morning working around the school—raking leaves, painting fences, whatever needed cleaning and fixing that season. We were enthusiastic to contribute such manual work in exchange for the brain reprieve. No one ever complained. The rhythm of the broom, rake or paintbrush was a welcome break from the rhythm of the pencil, slide rule and textbook. Plus the afternoon and evening blossomed into a wonderland of catch-up time.

Basking in warm memories such as this one was one of the few human activities still viable during January's frigid spell, along with gasping at terrifying weather maps and drooling over airline schedules to tropical climes.

Then a miraculous warm wind released the whole region. If the car didn't start on Monday at thirty below or Tuesday at twenty-seven below, it was washed and perfumed by a fifty degree soaring of spirits a few days later. On a thirty degree above zero weekend, Minnesotans acted like school kids with a surprise day off. Yessss!!!

If the freeways were jammed with angry, frozen commuters early in the week, Lake of the Isles was jammed with broomballers, skiers, joggers, walkers, ice fishers and skaters by the zillions on the toasty weekend. An entire urban population emerged from depression to celebrate sun, clean white snow and solid lake ice. Nature, the mother of all governors, had granted a timely January thaw.

Mrs. Coyote and I joined the throng strolling around the Lake. We drank in the sun on snow, the freshness of the air, the skaters, skiers, joggers and walkers.

"Yesss!!!" we exclaimed. "Yesss!!!"

This winter Mother Nature gave us her toughest shot in a decade if not a century. Yet not one person died. The frigid blast, although maddening, proved to be only inconvenient. The escape to warmth and sun, however, proved spectacular. Yesss!!!

Deadlines,
Dead Lines, Dead Lines

(March 1994)

Last night I worked until 2 a.m. I had no choice. I faced a deadline the next morning.

My late night didn't worry Mrs. Coyote. She was up until 4 a.m. working on a report due for a breakfast meeting.

All day she and I felt ragged and ugly. Why can't we manage our time better? Why do we let so much pile up against our deadlines? Wouldn't life be great without them?

In the middle of such a deadline attack, many people daydream.

Some imagine the rest of their lives lying on a beach in the sun, holding a drink that in turn holds a tiny umbrella, a novel open next to us upon the sand.

Others imagine themselves trekking from village to village

in the Himalayas, meeting the quiet folks and living simply on yak butter under the high blue curve of Mother Earth and the watchful white eye of Mt. Everest.

Others imagine an uncluttered life in a one room log cabin on an island on a lake next to the Boundary Waters Canoe Area—no electricity, no phone, no roads, no neighbors, no access to the mainland except by dogsled or canoe. Of course, no children.

Others see themselves simply turning off the TV at home, lighting a fire or grabbing a blanket and starting a slow, careful chewing on the tottering stack of unread books on the bedside table.

I dream about all of these. I can't choose among them. Of course, I don't have to. No deadline.

There's no hurry for me to get out the old trekking brochure or the new Louise Erdrich novel—hey, there's always tomorrow.

No need to start building the boat in the garage for the fantasy around-the-world voyage. I can work on the plans when I have more free time. Anyway, I haven't yet tied up all the cardboard stacked in the garage for recycling. No hurry. If I miss this week's pickup, there's always another one two weeks away.

Get the drift? Without deadlines, I'd be dead. I can't live without them.

Consider this column. The editor called today to remind me it is due tomorrow.

I groaned. Another near all-nighter loomed in front of me. Why, I sighed, why do I do this to myself?

Secretly, of course, I was enthralled. A deadline! Only one day to deliver an assignment means I can only put one day into it. I cannot fill weeks with research up to the last minute, or endlessly refine earlier drafts. In a day, this column will be finished. What a relief.

In real life, the worst projects I face are those without deadlines rather than those with them. I am a victim of Lenfestey's Law: the amount of time required to complete a project varies proportionately with the amount of time available to the final deadline.

It is a terrible curse, Lenfestey's Law. In college I worked all night before nearly every paper deadline and final examination. Not because I hadn't worked hard the previous weeks, but because there was always another document to read, another page to turn.

My adult life in teaching, communications and journalism is better. Yes, there is always another paper to grade, another source to call, another report to read, but there is always a deadline too, a clear signal that choices must be made and priorities accepted. The job will have a beginning, a middle, but also, thank heaven, an end.

Creative projects are the most frustrating. When is a poem, painting, song, short story or play finished? It can always be improved. Is two weeks too much to get it right? Twenty years?

Some years ago the poet Eve Merriam was asked how a poet knows when a poem is finished. She answered that she never does. However, she added, at some point the writer has to cut the work loose into the world and move on. "Cut your losses," is how she put it.

Her prescription is wise and sensible. Why then can't I follow it? That's easy. No deadline.

So deadlines are a god as well as a devil, in spite of the stress from them, the late nights, the exhaustion. Like right now, as I slowly push down the keys for this column, my fingers heavy with sleep.

I am running, easily, sweat glistening on my shoulders in the sun. I am moving toward a palm-lined horizon. The waves slowly roll onto the shore and splash my bare feet as I run. There is no end. I am barely touching the sand and sea, floating. My mind thrills to its growing calm. The sea glitters, salt sweat tingles my eyes, salt and kelp flavor the air. I float off the beach, striding over the horizon of palms, reefs and cerulean sea, accompanied now by leaping dolphins. We run and swim and soar together, the dolphins and I, through white innocent clouds, at perfect play, heart to dolphin heart, fellow spirits of the sea and air, totally alive.

I look down. I see my fingers flying over keys on a keyboard. In front of me a dream is captured in a cloud of brilliant pixels. Immediately ahead, a deadline looms. Yes! Without that requirement, this dream would have disappeared into the business end of sunrise.

Life without deadlines, the greatest of fantasies, would be the dullest of realities. Our awareness of the final, firm Dead Line teaches us that. And I don't mean waiting for Grateful Dead concert tickets. I mean Death, the Dead Line that animates the life line by creating consciousness of an ending. Since there is an end, we'd better get something done in the meantime. Make something new. Fix something old. Build a business. Clean up after yourself. Raise a child or four. Climb a mountain, raft a river, read a novel, paint a picture, write a poem. Finish this column. Perhaps it will have dolphins in it, flying through the sky.

Reading *Walden*

(April 1994)

My reading group assigned ourselves Henry David Thoreau's *Walden* for fall reading. Our plan was to discuss it at the north woods cabin of one of the members, the way we had traveled to Sauk Center, Sinclair Lewis's hometown, to discuss *Main Street* in the old hotel at the corner of Main Street and Sinclair Lewis Avenue.

Changed plans among the group's six members scotched the only workable fall weekend so we agreed to meet the second weekend in January. We would leave town right after Saturday breakfast, drive five hours north to the wilderness cabin, fire up the wood stove, cross country ski, cook dinner, discuss *Walden* over the dinner table, ski the next morning and return home the following evening.

I was enthusiastic to read as an adult this masterpiece of American literature, yet, as a parent and committed community member, a bit skeptical as well. Thoreau's premise—living alone self-sufficiently in the wilderness—I knew to be somewhat tainted. During his isolation, he reportedly leeched a bit off Ralph Waldo Emerson and other friends in nearby Concord. In addition, Thoreau never married, having been spurned, sadly, by the father of his intended. Without a lover, children and the multitude of consequent obligations, Thoreau's decision to devote 26 months of his life to self-sufficient solitude seems not as heroic as it first appears.

Still, when I began reading, I was enthralled by Thoreau's craft and wisdom. Reading *Walden* was like slowly plowing a rocky field and turning up chunk after chunk of pure gold.

I took notes, underlined, pulled quotes. I'd savor it, a sentence, a paragraph at a time. I'd fall asleep with it folded on my chest.

In spite of the slow going, I felt certain I could finish *Walden* in the calm after the busy Christmas holidays. But family and community cataclysms intervened in the form of a serious car accident involving our son and daughter-in-law prior to the holidays, and my position as coach of our 12-year-old daughter's basketball team, the WESAC Flames.

Anxiety over the accident sucked all life and time from our household until prognoses finally turned fully positive around New Year's Day. By then the WESAC Flames were desperately in need of every practice session I could wangle.

When the league basketball schedule arrived in the mail in early January, I winced as I read that the opening game would be played on Saturday, January 15, the same day as the rescheduled *Walden* meeting. How could I not coach the girls' first game? Yet how could I again change the reading group's plans?

On the Tuesday before the appointed Saturday, I was only 30 pages into *Walden* out of 221 in my edition. We were to leave at 8 o'clock Saturday morning. I said to myself that I would read 50 pages a night prior to departure while seeking a substitute coach. However, Tuesday evening disappeared into a practice of the WESAC Flames, Wednesday evening into an extended business meeting, Thursday into a non-profit board meeting.

Thursday night my back muscles, tight as violin strings, screamed at me to drop part of my load. I sheepishly called the reading group organizer to say that I simply could not attend the weekend trip. He responded that another of the six members had just dropped out too, needing a minor operation, so the rest would certainly be happy to reschedule. What a relief!

We set a third date, this time the second Saturday in March, the first free weekend after the end of the girls' basketball season.

The WESAC Flames learned useful life lessons that season—for example that poor preparation (many had never bounced a basketball before), inadequate practice time and too many outside obligations (half the team missed practices or games due to conflicts with music lessons, baby-sitting or Girl Scouts) can lead to a lack of success on the scoreboard. But over the course of the season the girls played with improved skill and teamwork and consistent good cheer. After the last game I threw a party at our house to honor our collective spiritual triumph.

The following Saturday morning the reading group crowded into a van for the five-hour drive north. We talked a lot on the drive, but no one brought up *Walden*. I certainly didn't, as I had read only to page 134.

As we turned down the dirt logging road toward the cabin, a sign celebrated the planting in 1965 of 15,000 Norway pines during a big family reunion, a grove now 30 feet tall.

The cabin was not much more than one simple room. It was built by our friend's grandparents as a pioneer homestead in 1902 on a budget, I imagine, not much greater than Thoreau's in 1845. As with most homesteads in the far north of short growing seasons, fragile topsoil and long, frigid winters, farming proved impractical. The family quickly dispersed into paying jobs in nearby iron mining towns, but managed to hang on to the old place as cleared fields returned to aspen, birch and ultimately planted pine, a succession similar to what takes place naturally after a forest fire.

We lit the wood stove and put on the stew pot, then skied over snow-covered pine needles to an open beaver pond. Two of us skied further east through the woods to the end of a snowmobile trail. On our return, the sky turned magenta and gold above the thick rim of trees. Sunset and the rhythm of my arms and legs skating over late season snow made me feel as if a glacial weight was melting off me, my spirit springing back to life with the earth.

Under the light of kerosene lamps, we ate a late dinner of thick stew and homemade bread while toasting the Gods and each other with plentiful red wine. We washed the dishes with water we had earlier pumped from the town well, then heated on the stove. Then we fell into bed like stones, without once bringing up *Walden.*

The next morning after a delicious skillet breakfast we skied again, this time west along another snowmobile trail through the woods. In the melting snow of nascent spring, we followed the faint imprints and occasional scat of timber wolves. We emerged from the woods at a huge swath carved through the wilderness for a powerline transporting electricity from massive hydroelectric dams in Ontario and Manitoba to energy-hungry industries and neighborhoods to the south. The clearing turned the heavily wooded landscape into a vista of dark granite ridges and open sky, a country where wolves feel at home but humans and electric power only pass through.

As we glided back along the trail, the morning sun softened the earth. The trail melted behind us, disappearing for another season.

At noon, we packed to go. We had not yet discussed

Walden, instead living a full Walden day as spring glided tentatively into the north woods.

On the drive home, we finally began, tentatively, to discuss Thoreau's experiences at Walden Pond. It turned out all of us had had unusual difficulty finding any time for private reading. Two fessed up to skimming several sections. I confessed that I was nearly one hundred pages shy of completion. All of us had been preoccupied with our jobs, health problems, family and community obligations, plus a vague anxiety that our hectic lives were spinning out of control. We agreed that this one-day visit to a 92-year-old north woods homestead had offered us the chance to reclaim the rhythm and majesty of the natural world and we all felt much more at peace.

Turning from the rough back roads onto the smooth freeway and heading south, we took turns reading out loud to each other *Walden's* celebrated concluding chapter.

During his last spring at Walden Pond, Thoreau lay on the ground next to a sand bank and watched a rivulet begin again to move the fluids of the earth, grain by grain.

> *"A single rain makes the grass many shades greener. So our prospects brighten on the influx of better thoughts. We should be blessed if we lived in the present always, and took advantage of every accident that has befell us, like the grass which confesses the influence of the slightest dew that falls on it; and did not spend our time atoning for the neglect of past opportunities, which we call doing our duty. We loiter in winter while it is already spring."*

As we drove south, reading and talking, the winter landscape turned green around us.

Sometime this spring I will finish reading *Walden*. It will be a joy, not a duty. My particular winter accidents—of crunched metal, fractured bones and frozen hoops—have thawed naturally to green, miraculous rivulets. Planted and tended as best one can, one's life proceeds as always, in its own time.

> *"I learned this, at least, by my experiment; that if one advances confidently in the direction of his dreams, and endeavors to live the life which he has imagined, he will meet with a success unexpected in common hours. He will put some things behind, will pass an invisible boundary. . . . In proportion as he simplifies his life, the laws of the universe will appear less complex, and solitude will not be solitude, nor poverty poverty, nor weakness weakness. If you have built castles in the air, your work need not be lost; that is where they should be. Now put the foundations under them."*

Thoreau turned what life offered him, solitude, into a foundation for the inspired dream he realized at Walden Pond. Those of us wedded instead to family build from that foundation the ceremonies of children, the rituals of work and community, the rites of old age. In the nature of one's own place, in the hoop of one's own time, one builds a castle in the air as well as on the ground. It is only important to build one. Whether the foundation or the castle comes first is not important.

The Wall of Hope

(May 1994)

This June our youngest child will graduate from the sixth grade at Kenwood School and break our hearts. She is the last of our four children to attend Kenwood, beginning 21 years ago when teacher Jackie Bray welcomed our eldest son into the second grade the year we moved here.

Jackie Bray initiated our family into the mysteries of the Minneapolis public schools. She and a long list of inspired teachers and volunteers at Kenwood not only loved the minds of our four children but also nurtured their hearts and spirits. Because the teachers did their job with such care and conviction, our job as parents was immeasurably easier.

In our long tenure as school parents, we have seen Kenwood School undergo numerous physical transformations.

In our early years, Mrs. Coyote and other parents battled ferociously when the School Board slated Kenwood for closure due to nose-diving enrollment in the Minneapolis district. The parents won and Kenwood instead was renovated and modernized, including a new recreation center and gymnasium attached to the school, the first such collaboration between the school district and the park board in the city.

When city voters supported a 1991 citywide referendum question providing funds for a lower student-teacher ratio, a volunteer Kenwood parent-teacher committee creatively carved out the necessary additional classrooms.

Each year, PTA parents cooked spaghetti suppers, sold wrapping paper and otherwise cajoled money and commitment out of the community to spruce up classrooms and modernize the playground, finally installing new equipment.

Though the building has changed, the essential educational experience has not. Dedicated teachers still take a family's offspring and guide them to the end of sixth grade, the brink of adolescence. And since the desegregation mandates of the early 1970s, the student population has been well integrated racially and economically, split about evenly between students of color and whites, middle-class and lower income families.

Still, something profound has changed in students' lives during our time as Kenwood parents. I learned what it was when I visited the "Wall of Hope."

In honor of Martin Luther King's birthday, teachers, administrators and volunteers encouraged students, parents, teachers and visitors to inscribe a personal statement of hope on a yellow rectangular piece of paper. The rectangle was then taped over a brick near the entrance to the school under a large sign, "Wall of Hope." The goal was to reflect the hope that the school has for each child and that each child has for the future.

Visiting school one day, I was commandeered by a parent volunteer to add my own "brick." I've forgotten now what I added to that wall, but I'll never forget what I read there. What I found was both hopeful and dismaying.

Naturally, dreams of good fortune were well represented: "I hope for good grades and one million dollars." "I hope to get tickets to the basketball games."

Many students sensibly hoped for a useful vocation: "veterinarian," "jump rope player," "baseball player," "woman president," "policeman," "basketball player," "lawyer," "college graduate and engineer," "doctor," "pilot," "scientist," "Kenwood teacher."

Such sentiments are probably similar to those of any of

the classes of children who attended Kenwood throughout its 101-year history. And hopes for planetary progress demonstrated a sense of social and environmental responsibility probably new and certainly admirable in citizens so young: "End world poverty." "I wish all people would keep our earth clean." "I dream the pollution will stop." "I dream that all children get a good education." "Help the poor." "I wish that all homeless have a home."

But along with such practical dreams and generous spirit, the Wall of Hope held much bleaker notes, demonstrating a frightening first hand knowledge of chaos and pain. Listen:

"I wish they would stop shooting and stabbing." "I wish that people would stop robbing and killing each other." "I hope people don't get killed." "I hope young people will be safe." "I wish that there would be no color for skin so that everyone would be the same." "I hope that people stop killing." "I hope that people stop living in pain." "I hope my Dad gets out of jail soon." "I wish that young people will grow up in safe houses, safe neighborhoods, safe schools." "I hope that every young person grows up with someone like a mom who loves them and takes care of them." "I hope all young people grow up in a home." "I wish no fighting." "I wish no white person would see a black person coming toward them and run." "I wish there was not violence in my life."

"I had a dream that all people will be together," wrote one young student. *Had* a dream? Certainly she simply misused the tense. Her dream couldn't have died sometime before the end of sixth grade. Could it?

Kenwood School did not produce this fear and chaos, nor did any teacher. To the contrary, the Kenwood staff works harder than ever to keep student dreams alive. Teachers spend hundreds of dollars a year out of their own pockets to buy small necessities that students used to bring with them — pencils, paper, books, socks, parkas. They drive students to school after parents divorce, or move across town, or disappear. They console students too terrified to enter the classroom because this was the fifth move to a new school in a year. They comfort the far too many children who are afraid when they go *home*, not when they go to school.

No, the schools did not fail. Families have failed. Communities have failed. Society has failed.

"I love Kenwood School," Mayor Sharon Sayles-Belton wrote on her brick on the Wall of Hope. So does my family. All our four children, and we as parents, enthusiastically recommend Kenwood to other families as an exceptional and hopeful institution of learning, friendship, care and community. The children arrive every year with bright shining eyes, and the school brings oxygen to the fire for learning within them. Our hearts break at the prospect of losing Kenwood from our lives after so many years.

Our hearts break too over the broken lives trailing like shadows behind too many Kenwood children. The "Wall of Hope" represents both our children's promise and their frightened, frightening reality. Resolving their hopelessness is Mayor Sayles-Belton's greatest challenge. And yours. And mine.

Why Hair Turns White with Age

(July 1994)

My neighbor sports a distinguished topping of jet-exhaust white hair. He is also deservedly famous as a man of wisdom. I argue that the two are related.

As one who at nearly 50 years of age has a beard now fully white but a head almost entirely not so, I am about halfway toward my right to pontificate on this matter. Halfway has never stopped me in the past, nor will it now. So here, for your edification, is my theory of why human hair turns white with age.

If you believe that white hair is just accidental, like crooked teeth or bad breath or corns, think again. Humans of all races get it, as do our ape and chimpanzee cousins. That means natural selection must hold some advantage for ape-like creatures with a disposition toward hair whitened with age. What could it be?

As a species evolved from swinging through trees, humans absorb essential information primarily through sight rather than smell or touch or hearing. Hair color is visual information. What does it communicate?

Imagine an Australopithecus adolescent woman strolling over the veldt. She comes upon a band of Australopithecus guys hanging out at the Baobab Tree Cafe. One has white hair, the others dark. What does she know right away?

The white-haired guy has the most experience, right? So he is the one to go to for the important questions. Should I marry? Is Visa better than American Express? College or technical school? Rent or buy? Should we care if professional basketball leaves the city? Should I organize a neighborhood block party? Poetry or prose?

He knows the answers. He has already made most of the mistakes life offers and survived to tell what he has learned. He's the wise guy.

Second, the young woman knows instantly that the white-haired guy is not an appropriate sexual partner. Too old. Weak. Feeble. Pathetic. Boring. Nearly fifty. Gross!

Think about it. I sure have.

At 49, I feel and look as good as I ever have (well, I wasn't so great when I was younger either). I'm virile, witty, and can play basketball better than when I was eighteen (well, I wasn't so great then either). So what if my memory malfunctions occasionally and I can't remember a friend's name or where I hid the car keys (in my hand) or where the hell are my glasses (on my head), that's only because my brain is stuffed so full of valuable experiences.

Here's something I do know: Growing older does not narrow a male's interest in the opposite sex. On the contrary, instead of finding only one's peer group attractive, as is the case with teenagers, I now find virtually all women alluring and fascinating, from sixteen to seventy-six. No, eighty-six, no, ninety-six.

But young women don't see me this way at all. When I walk down the street in the Uptown neighborhood, I can't help but scope out with my peripheral vision the delightful passing parade of urban pulchritude. However, I never get a foxy return glance from the teens and twenty-somethings. To them I look as useful as a white-bearded stop sign.

Instead, the younger women eagerly check out their male peers, all rebels-without-a-clue as far as I can tell, wearing comically oversize pants and multiple earrings. Older women too are checking out the younger guys (and each other, by the way, but that's another story).

Of course I would never act inappropriately on my glancing interest—I'm a fully socialized member of the adult community after all—but even if I truly wanted to, I would be stymied by the obvious lack of interest.

Case in point. Last weekend I emerged from the Boundary Waters Canoe Area after three exhilarating days camping with my 22-year-old son. We stopped at a small restaurant along the north shore of Lake Superior on the way home.

I felt fit as a fiddle after three days of paddling and carrying canoes. My son, on the other hand, looked unkempt, slouching and loutish, smelling of campfires and fish. Yet the college-aged waitress, cute as a bug's ear as my father used to say, looked past me like a tree stump in the trail while her eyes worked him over like a punching bag.

I'm amazed she brought me black coffee. Yet I understood.

Younger women don't see white-haired men as viable romantic partners for a simple reason: We're not. We're too old.

But we do have experience. We've been around the block so many times we know where the curbs are. We've known life without TV, McDonalds and espresso. We can tell you what a loan application looks like and if you should sign it. We've experienced birth and death, marriage and divorce, success and failure, war and peace, job interviews, car salesmen, car accidents, insurance adjusters, hospitals, PTA, children's college applications, septic tank overflows, garden slugs, health insurance forms, highway construction, bad maps, bad medicine, bad teachers, bad waiters, bad actors, bad writers.

If the young waitress had bothered to ask, I would have happily advised her to consult her elders before she marries the first age-appropriate lout who looks up at her and licks his lips.

I've earned the whiteness in this beard. No way will I respond to the pervasive advertisements urging males of my generation to "take the white out" with a coloring shampoo.

Hell, I'd probably have to fight off the young ladies again. And no one would ask me for my advice. Both situations would be a terrible waste of my true skills and experience.

Is Daylight Savings Time a Metaphor?

(November 1994)

Spring ahead, fall back. Lose an hour in the spring, gain an hour in the fall. Is Daylight Savings Time a metaphor?

I love that resurrected hour every fall. This year I feel I need an extra week, a year, a decade. Still, I am thrilled that time is handed out freely in October when one needs it most.

Someone once opined that time, like education, is wasted on the young. Indeed. Young people have taste buds but no taste. They are in a hurry but have no valuable place to go.

They don't linger over flavors but swill beer and inhale burgers while banging off each other and the world like bumper cars.

Now that I have lived half a century, turning toward my own fall, I remember that wasted springtime so clearly. That's why each day of this lingering, colorful season demands to be savored.

This particular October has been gilded with intensely warm light and color—the grass dark as evergreens, the deciduous leaves piled in mounds of yellow, russet, umber and tan along the neighborhood streets. Each afternoon, sunlight canting through clinging yellow maple leaves turns the crowns to golden lampshades along the boulevard.

I grow almost feverish, wanting to enter inside each color everyday. I swim nearly every evening in spring-fed Lake Harriet, clearest of the city lakes, until the water cools me.

One mid-October weekend I camped with my daughter and her best friend in the Boundary Waters Canoe Area, the nation's most accessible true wilderness. Dark green cedar and black spruce lined the granite shores of tannin-colored lakes. The birch, poplar and hardwood trees had all dropped their leaves, their bare branches weaving a misty, transparent halo on the surrounding hills. In sun and rain we canoed through silken air, smoked ourselves with fire, sang into the sparks, bottled the well water and brought it home.

The last Wednesday in October the family raked the latest fallen leaves that had gathered in huge but weightless piles under the elms and maples at our corner of Girard and Lincoln. In the process, we uncovered bright green grass supple and long as sea grass.

Wordsworth must have been thinking of the young when he wrote "The world is too much with us, late and soon,/ getting and spending, we lay waste our powers./ Little we see in nature that is ours." At fifty, I see glory in nature everywhere around me. It is the affairs of men that press with less weight this particularly brilliant season.

The global miseries that move and trouble us in the flicker of a television screen or headline pale when fall sunlight passes through golden leaves.

In the wide world people come and go talking of Sarajevo. In the neighborhood, sirens pierce the night. Yes, to forget the poor or abandon the war-torn would be a crime. Yet my soul this fall is insatiable for warm sunlight, pale blue sky, cool water, fire and food in the company of children. The sun this October, low in the sky, has lingered and warmed past all reason. Each day glows tan below blue like my skin and eyes.

This fall I am drawn to magazine articles on geology, not current events. I recently read that the glacial dunes of Lake Superior march a few feet a year, slowly engulfing trees, houses, even small towns. I find that pace of movement, grain by grain, attractive.

Is that the meaning of "fall back"? A falling off the overcrowded pace of hectic routines, a fall into focus on sharper colors when the arms of oak, the thighs of elms, the veins of still clinging maple leaves filter a blue so intense it may be the eye behind the sky?

So the days grow shorter, is that sad? Smaller portions rolled around the tongue like wine—swirled, not swilled— are languorous, naturally full, complex and long lasting.

My fall back in this my 50th year is to nature's grace, where the light is better, the air purer, the lake water more exhilarating. It is all I can do not to jump in— to piles of leaves, to chilling lakes—every minute of every fall day.

A High and Holy Calling

(December 1994)

I have always admired what the minister says when he returns the baby to its parents after baptism in front of our congregation: "May God go with you in the high and holy calling as parents of this child." What practical wisdom that phrase embodies. Parents definitely deserve baptism too as they enter the relentless commitment called parenthood, leading as it does to unimaginable joys, terrors and surprises. Consider this Thanksgiving weekend.

My calling was not high and holy as I yelled up the back stairs for the fourth time trying to wake my son the Sunday after Thanksgiving. Nor was I feeling high and holy as I finally threw water on his face. His night of pool playing with his old high school friends may have been fun. But the resulting two hours of sleep was less amusing at 7:30 a.m. with snow beginning to fall and a 9 a.m. plane to catch back to college.

The water in the face caused a stir, then the rough semblance of action. He managed to stumble into his clothes, collect the last of his laundry out of the dryer and stuff it into his duffel, then make the rounds of family hugs.

The airport was not yet crowded when we arrived at 8:30 a.m. As he checked his laundry bag, I hugged his burly body, pleased we could carve out Thanksgiving time together. Then he was gone.

Thanksgiving weekend, that calling together of families, finally tapered toward an exhausted and satisfying close.

Mrs. Coyote had used all her spare time for two weeks to prepare the house in anticipation of five families sharing the day with us. Two of our three adult children traveled home for the occasion. We were pleased, their little sister thrilled. We planned family as well as community activities for the long weekend.

I picked the kids up at the airport the day before Thanksgiving, one from New York, the other from Colorado.

They both proved helpful in Thanksgiving dinner preparations. All our children relish the task of peeling boiled chestnuts, a traditional ingredient in turkey stuffing. This amazes me, as fingernails hurt for days after peeling those hot, stubborn things. Peeling chestnuts around the kitchen table has become a revered family ritual, proving—as if proof were needed—that tradition triumphs over pain.

The stuffing tasted delicious when pulled from inside two cavernous turkeys on Thanksgiving afternoon. This fact was attested to by a flock of six families from the neighborhood including children aged three to twenty-four. Such abundant human presence at games, toasts, conversation, poetry and storytelling filled the day with a delighted, stuffed satisfaction.

The next morning the house was trashed. That's also part of the Thanksgiving ritual. Unfortunately, family clean-up helpers were as scarce as chestnut-peelers had been abundant. The same wonderful children who believed coming home for Thanksgiving the *sine qua non* of traditional values now remembered that partying every night with old high school friends was also a traditional value.

So parents spent Friday and half of Saturday swiping dish cloths over the accumulated piles of plates, glassware, bottles, platters, bowls, pans, pitchers, rental tables, cups, saucers and tablecloths. We took our time, and the experience was quite a pleasant one.

We did schedule a Saturday afternoon walk around the lake for the whole family. That would be the last chance for moderate exercise and family conversation before the maelstrom of departures back to school.

We hadn't counted on a homework crisis.

Early Saturday afternoon, our thirteen-year-old daughter suddenly remembered that she had a group project due on Tuesday for her seventh grade class. Group projects seem to present particular headaches for seventh graders because someone has to organize the group's disparate interests and schedules. That task had fallen, our daughter now remembered, on her.

Her brain seized. Her body grew heavy. Her head slumped to the kitchen table in stubborn despair. The weight of this unfamiliar task was too much for her to handle in the middle of Thanksgiving with her family.

Her parents became exasperated. After weeks working on—and completing—our Thanksgiving homework, the idea of finally getting OUT of the house was as exciting as the thought of Thanksgiving in it had been the week before. Fresh air was the high and holy calling we had in mind.

Big brother and big sister, two nights of hard partying behind them, rode to the rescue. While the eldest daughter took Mom for a brisk walk, big brother worked on the little one with his David Letterman style humor and eventually lifted her out of her funk.

After that the rest was easy. Big sister helped her call members of the project team and tell them to meet at our house at 4 p.m. on Sunday to assemble all the work. The project was under control. An afternoon of family time was shot, but the weekend of family harmony returned in a surprising, even high and holy way: the children had taken charge.

After dropping our son at the airport, I drove back home

very slowly on the icy freeway. I sang along to tapes of organ music and opera left in my car by our eldest daughter. The music – new to me – was gloriously inspiring.

In the peace and quiet of church later that morning, I witnessed a baptism ceremony. Six families—like those at our house Thanksgiving Day—stood together holding wriggling, regally wrapped new babies in their arms. I grinned at the sturdy, hopeful parents, shared their joy, their commitment, whatever maddening crises big and small their future is sure to hold. I ate the bread. I drank the wine. I gave thanks. Outside, extraordinary lightning and thunder crashed while heavy snows fell.

And when my car got stuck in the driveway as I returned home, I could only get it out with the family and neighbors pushing together.

PART FIVE

DEJA VU
ALL OVER AGAIN

1995-96

Finding a Father
in the Neighborhood

(February 1995)

Several months ago one of our oldest neighborhood friends asked me to review a letter she was about to send to the father of her only child. She needed help getting the tone just right, she said, for the situation was a bit dicey. Her son is twenty-seven years old, yet the father has no idea he exists. Ok, I said, come on over.

The letter was addressed to her son's grandfather, the only relative she had been able to trace after an intensive search for the father spanning seven years.

I drew a deep breath. Where does one learn how to ask an elderly man to inform his son that he has a child unknown to him from his distant past?

My friend's letter spelled out forthrightly why she needed to contact the father. Her own son, now grown, had become intensely curious as a young adult about his biological parentage. He pushed his mother hard to find his father. They did not want money from the father, only contact. She enclosed her address and phone number plus a description of her son, his address and phone number in California where he now lived and worked, plus a photograph of him to give her story a human face.

I found the tone of her letter just right and encouraged her to send it. We then sat around the kitchen table as she told me her story.

The letter begins the last chapter of a story that began on a city bus in Minneapolis twenty-eight years before.

He had been home on leave from Viet Nam. They met riding downtown and liked each other. They dated. Once she visited his parents with him in a northern suburb. Then he shipped back to Viet Nam. When she found that she was pregnant she immediately wrote him a letter. She never received a reply. His first and last names were common and she was not sure she properly located him in the Army. Finally, after giving up on a reply, she tried to contact the parents she had once visited. But they had moved out of state in the meantime and she could get no forwarding address. As the coup de grace, Army representatives told her that servicemen were exempt from paternity suits.

Young and poor, she fatalistically accepted her situation, delivering her baby alone in a Minneapolis hospital. She moved into a small one-bedroom apartment in our neighborhood where she raised her son until he left home to seek his fortune in California at twenty-one.

As I let her out the front door, I watched her familiar form stride toward her home two blocks away, the letter in her hand. She mailed it the next day.

When we moved here twenty-three years ago, one of the first sounds we heard was a maddening rattle from the plastic wheels of a "Big Wheel" tricycle rumbling up and down the sidewalk in front of our new apartment. The driver was a wildly energetic seven-year-old boy. Our oldest son, also seven, sat on the front steps and watched him ride up and down. Soon they made friends and, in the neighborhood way, my wife and I became friends with his mother as well. We visited often between their apartment around the corner on Franklin Avenue and ours on Fremont Avenue. When we moved away for two years to Massachusetts, they took the bus to visit us. When we returned, they welcomed us home.

Over the years, we slowly learned the outlines of the story of this independent-minded woman and her only child. She was raised in St. Paul in a large Irish Catholic family that numbered a famous prizefighter in its lineage. She lived largely on disability payments from the state due to her ongoing struggle with asthma and epilepsy, although she eventually earned a nursing degree. We knew her publicly as a fierce and effective protector of the neighborhood against all threats real and imagined, especially from bureaucrats in City Hall or homeowners in the neighborhood who forgot to take renters' interests into account. Her son's father was never mentioned and we never asked.

At nineteen, however, her son finally did ask her, pushing to find out what he could about his father. Wary of opening this long-closed box and skeptical that she would find anything useful inside, she nevertheless agreed to try.

After seven years of dead ends, last spring she remembered that her boyfriend's father was a member of a union. She contacted the local union office and was given an address in Detroit. She sent him a letter before the one she showed me but received no reply.

She finally phoned the Detroit office where he worked. His former secretary informed her that the gentleman had retired several years before. No, she would not give a forwarding address. My friend decided to try one last time. She marked the second envelope "personal."

It turned out that the grandfather had received the first letter and decided he should do nothing with the information. His son was happily married with two grown daughters. What could possibly be gained from contact with an unknown child of an unknown mother? And what if the woman's story was not real?

The grandfather was not at home the day the forwarded letter arrived at his house in Detroit that Saturday. His wife and her granddaughter saw the envelope and thought something might need immediate attention. When they opened the envelope, a young man's photograph fell to the floor. As the grandmother picked it up, she immediately recognized a member of her family. Her granddaughter shrieked, "This is my brother!" Without waiting for the grandfather or husband to come home, they immediately picked up the phone and called their new brother at the California phone number listed in the letter.

That night the son called his mother's apartment. "Mom," he said, "I just had a call from my sister."

That was six months ago.

The father proved amazed and gladdened he had a son, a boon he never thought he'd have. Far from seeing this discovery as a problem, he wanted make up for lost time. The father, sister and stepmother flew to California to meet the son.

But let the son now carry on the tale. He called me last week to tell what this change in his life has brought him.

"Confusion. I didn't need a father, I thought. I had the neighborhood families of my friends. I got pieces of all of you. I got to be who I was. You all let me do that.

"Still, at nineteen I really felt I wanted to know my biological father. Before that I had never asked my Mom, but I pushed her hard since twenty.

"I never thought I'd meet him. I thought I was safe. Twenty-seven years of believing I'd never meet my father. Now I've found him. His whole family wants me to be part of them. My sisters have written me letters.

"He wants to give me money to make up for all those years. He's a truck driver. I can't take it. I hated being on welfare. I'm not going to take any now.

"So... a happy ending? More like a strange beginning. Will it work out? We'll see. I think so."

The fathers of his neighborhood friends were surprised to hear the role he believes we played in his life. We always saw him as a cheerful, energetic and loyal friend. We still talk on the phone, write and visit, as do our sons. He recently returned for our son's wedding. That's just what long time neighbors do.

And we aren't fooled either by his compliment. His feisty, determined mother brought him up, with significant help from her family and the state. She gave back to the community bountifully by fiercely protecting her son and the neighborhood in which they both lived. She would face down any official or community leader who didn't actively maintain our mutual home. She even had the courage, finally, to complete the story of her son's immaculate birth when that too was needed of her, although she feared losing the child she had so fiercely protected.

She didn't lose him, of course. He just added another family to the one he grew up with in their apartment on Franklin Avenue and in the neighborhood.

Deja Vu All Over Again

(August 1995)

There I was at 10:45 p.m. on a Saturday night struggling to think of what I could write about for the September issue. I already missed the regular and backup deadlines, with the ultimate, final, drop dead typesetter's deadline looming only a day away, yet I was stymied for a topic. Nothing would break loose. Every idea seemed suspended in time.

Then the phone rang. It was our eldest son calling from his home in New Mexico, sounding blissfully tired. "Hello, Dad," he said. "Well, I guess you are a grandfather."

So that's the story I've been waiting for. I am a grandfather.

He told me I am a grandfather thanks to the magnificent performance by his extraordinarily strong wife only two years after breaking her neck in a frightening car accident. She masterfully endured 17 hours of difficult labor before introducing to the world a 7 pound, 15 ounce boy, healthy and mysterious.

Instantly I remembered this son's, our first child's, birth 28 years ago and my awe at my wife's strength as she pushed him into life.

My son said the baby has the long Lenfestey family upper lip, though he's not sure exactly what that is. I replied that when he was born we noticed the same lip on him, even though we didn't know what it was either. "I know the story," he said.

"The birth was harder than we thought it would be," he said. He described the long, stalled labor, the final trip down the hall to prepare for an emergency cesarean section if needed (it wasn't), all of it far more difficult than their birth classes had led them to believe. "Same with us," I said, "28 years ago."

He said the baby was in a posterior position, so the doctor finally had to use forceps to help him turn. "You were turned with forceps too," I said. "I know," he said.

I recalled that his head was shaped like a football at birth. He said his new baby has that football head, too. "It will round out in a few weeks," I said. "Yours did." "I know," he said.

He said the baby was in the room with them now, an entirely new experience for them of sharing space with a third living creature. I remembered what that was like for us, when we fixed up a closet in our graduate school apartment for him to sleep in. "This is just the beginning," I said. "Your youngest sister, feeling ill, slept in our bed just last night." "I understand," he said.

Although they have known for months that the baby was to be a boy, given the magic of ultrasound, they still couldn't decide on a name. "Same with us with your brother," I said. "I know the story," he said.

The two new parents were very tired after the all night labors. "Time for you to sleep," I said. "Yes," he said.

Then I heard a sound, something forgotten yet familiar. "Well," my son said, "the baby just woke up." He reached out the receiver so I could hear that sound, a cross between a cackling laugh and a frightened cry. His beginning. Our next step. "Hello," I said to my grandson, "welcome to planet Earth." I said to my son, "I remember that sound." "Me too, when my youngest sister was born," he said. "By the way," he said, "you use that 'welcome to planet Earth' line on every new baby you see, don't you?" "Yes," I said. "It's a good one," he said.

"There is bad news," he said. "Yes?" I answered, suddenly anxious. "I watched part of the Vikings' exhibition football game while we waited at the hospital. They were terrible." "I know," I said, "your brother was at the game. It was ugly."

"I love you, Dad. " "I love you, son, and daughter-in-law, and new baby grandson." "Good night." "Good night."

So that is the topic that was delivered unto me this August 25th, 1995 for the first paper of the fall. A phone rang in the heart of night, when one's fears about the risks of parenthood run highest. We have had those calls. Others have had those calls. But there are also late night calls of pure exhausted wonder and joy. For the chance to write about such glad tidings, I am extremely grateful.

Intruders in the Night

(September 1995)

Five blocks away, a neighbor woke in midnight blackness, his wife screaming. The intruder had returned, she screamed again. This time he's right outside the bedroom door!

The previous night his wife had called him at his business hotel, terrified. An intruder stalked the first floor, she said. She had shined a flashlight into the darkness, but he escaped before she could stop him. Her husband calmed her from long distance as best he could, not sure she wasn't dreaming.

Tonight she wasn't. Tonight he could hear the intruder entering the bathroom right next to the bedroom, accompanied by a loud splashing.

Splashing?

Yes, splashing. Welcome to your worst bathroom nightmare—a rat emerging from the toilet.

The previous night it swam out of the first floor toilet, then escaped down same. Tonight it was crawling out of the second floor toilet.

The husband jumped out of bed and ran to slam the toilet lid before it scaled the bowl. Too late. The rat was already on the floor. It looked up, dripping: beady red eyes, sharp yellow incisors, wet matted fur, long naked tail.

The husband slammed the toilet lid so it couldn't duplicate yesterday's escape, then slammed the bathroom door to trap him inside. Meanwhile his wife called the exterminator, who refused to visit until morning.

The rat skritch-skritched at the bathroom door the rest of the night trying to get into the bedroom, an escape strategy totally unacceptable to the two humans involved. One or both of them got out of bed every half-hour or so and pounded on the bathroom door, keeping the rat at bay for a while before it resumed its skritching.

As bleary-eyed dawn grayed the eastern sky, an exterminator pushed the doorbell chime. He set traps around the bedroom, then slowly opened the bathroom door. No rat. He hunted everywhere. No rat. The toilet seat was still down. Had the rat lifted the lid, climbed back in, then politely closed it for the next customer as proper parent rats should have taught it?

It hadn't. Just as the exterminator turned to leave the bathroom, the rat jumped up out of the wastebasket right next to his leg!

The exterminator quickly recovered and chased the rat around and around the bedroom, finally toward a trap. Snap, dead nightmare. The rat was buried without ceremony in a city garbage can.

For these beleaguered neighbors, the elation of victory proved short-lived. Their bathroom, that bastion of private and necessary acts such as reading the entire Sunday newspaper, had lost its sense of sanctuary.

When the neighbor told me the story, I immediately recognized his tormentor as the relatively common, landfill-variety Norway rat. About the size of a guinea pig, it is a shy, resourceful animal. Were it not nocturnal, one might consider it no more a pest than a gray squirrel. Then again, maybe not.

The rat apparently entered the house through a cracked underground sewer line, then climbed up inside the pipes, a quite unusual occurrence. After several weeks of digging, several thousand dollars and several bouts of constipation, our neighbors solved their intruder problem.

Although of little comfort to our bathroom-afflicted neighbors, their story hardly represents the worst involving rat intruders in the neighborhood. For a truly big deal, try sewer rats. Big as dogs with long matted fur and no fear of humans, they are lumbering behemoths of frightening omnipotence.

Hushed city pest inspectors and plumbers have told me stories of hysterical midnight phone calls emanating from households violated by convoys of arrogant sewer rats. Norway rats at least stand back when you pound on the door. Sewer rats think you want them to join you in bed.

Fortunately, sewer rat visits are easily preventable. Never let toilet bowls drain dry, unfortunately an all-too-common occurrence with forgotten basement toilets in the old houses in this neighborhood. Without a water seal, sewer rats will pay a visit to our delightfully varied neighborhood. If you don't leave the water window open, they seem quite willing to remain in the cozy subterranean neighborhood below this one. They dine well, I am told, on the abundance of our garbage disposals.

Then, of course, there are the frightening encounters with large human intruders. One friend a few blocks away recently woke in the middle of the night as an uninvited gentleman caller was going through her underwear drawer. She screamed and her brave husband rolled on top of her to protect her. The intruder ran out. The next morning her husband said he was sound asleep and didn't remember a thing.

No question, however, which are the most consistent midnight miscreants in this or any neighborhood: Children. They rob parents of sleep nearly nightly. Babies cry from hunger, teenagers groan from algebra frustration, proto-adults scream at deadlines for college applications. Then one day they coolly walk out the door to college. "Don't worry about us, Mom and Dad," they say. "We'll sleep on that," parents wearily respond.

But at least these are intruders you asked for. They may wreck your nights but they make your days.

Moving Memories from the Old House

(October 1995)

After 48 years at the same address, my mother decided to move out of the old house. At 87, she felt could no longer do justice to the gardens that were her challenge and her love, nor could she tolerate the highway department's decision to widen her street one more time, shaving off still more of her front yard.

Her decision represented a remarkable change of heart from her sensible stance only a few years before. No way she would ever move. Heck, let the kids deal after her death with a lifetime in which nothing was ever thrown away.

Although my two sisters and I never pushed, we were glad she changed her mind, but when the house sold right away we were shocked by the swiftness. Mother had imagined a whole winter to winnow and pack her accumulated treasures and detritus. Instead, she had eight weeks.

Soon after the sale, her friends young and old arrived to help her attack the mountain of packing. One immediately began taking old paintings, prints and photographs off the walls, some of which hadn't been disturbed since Mother and Dad moved to the house 48 years before from two blocks away.

Stop! Mother sat down, shaken. They were going too fast. She realized that she wanted, she needed, photographs taken of every room in the house, for her, for all of us, to remember. The house and my mother stood still over the next few days until a photographer froze the memories into separate books for her and her three children.

My two sisters soon arrived from out of town to help with the project. On the weekends, I drove over to help as well.

One sister worked with my mother every day for two weeks. She well understood both the urgency of the deadline and Mother's desire to savor every memory. She threw out cartons of mouse-eaten minutes from Wisconsin League of Women Voter meetings, piles of underlined scripts from community theater plays and file folder after file folder of ancient fund-raising college records, but she saved even the smallest scrap that sparked Mother to personal and family memories. And that was a lot of stuff.

The house held the accumulated possessions of nearly 50 years of marriage, including her wedding dress and his military uniform, all our elementary school report cards and every letter we had every written home. In addition, as the surviving matriarch of two extensive clans, Mother stuffed every closet, attic drawer and basement storeroom with family and regional history.

In an upstairs bureau we found a musty collection of photographs dating from the mid-nineteenth century. Only Mother could still identify any of the plainly-dressed pioneers from the beginning of modern Wisconsin history. My sister and I eagerly wrote down the names.

At the bottom of another drawer photographs turned up that no one remembered ever having seen before. They showed the new house my father's parents built in 1922 right across the street. That find was particularly spectacular since an old high school friend had recently bought the house and had written me only a few weeks earlier wondering if we had any photographs to guide him in restoration.

My sister and I took time out from packing boxes to walk across the street to give him the photographs. The physical act of walking that childhood route called up memories lodged deep in our bones. Every Sunday after church, the family walked to our grandparents' house for Sunday dinner. Dressed in scratchy formal clothes, we passed the vacant lot, the lilac hedge, the wall grandfather built from chunks of old pavement. Inside, grandfather loudly sharpened the carving knife while grandmother officiated over a room brimming with cousins, the air heavy with the scent of roast beef, Yorkshire pudding and gravy. So sharp the memories, yet grandfather died when I was four, my sister five.

Two bundles of old love letters turned up. One was letters to my mother from the man to whom she was engaged prior to meeting our father. The other was my wife's letters to me during our college courtship.

I did not witness my mother's reaction to her discovery. My sister tells that in untying the stack of letters wrapped in a ribbon, mother entered a space in her life profoundly important and profoundly private. She revealed to my sister part of that story as they read several letters and wept together. I do not know all the details, except to understand that there are stories best kept tied in ribbons and a right time to tell them.

Alone in my bedroom where I had slept from the age of three until I left home after college, I found the small wooden box holding letters from the college girlfriend who was to become my wife. I sat on the bed under which ravenous monsters once lurked and read two of them. The paper fairly crackled with her passionate writing. I crackled with it, struck weak with fresh romantic feeling.

When I returned home, I brought my family a welter of small discoveries. I was bursting to show them the teething ring with my name and tooth marks on it. My daughters instead reached for the wooden box of letters. No, I heard myself saying. Not yet. Not, at least, until I have had more time to spend with them in private.

Was I afraid that the letters might contain something inappropriate for their eyes? You bet. Far more important, they recorded moments meant to be private, young love preserved like a fly in amber. I felt the rush to privacy all over again, like an army recruit eagerly tearing open a letter from a hometown lover, then seeking out a private place in the trenches in which to read it. Like perfume from a pharaoh's tomb, the letters concentrated in the nostrils, losing nothing over time.

My experience with my old love letters was a microcosm of what my mother must have felt each day as she sorted through her past—her mother's wedding china, fifty years of Christmas cards, letters written by her husband to her children, the children's letters back, letters written by lifelong friends to her after his funeral.

The attic closets were bursting with her magnificent costume collection, initially gathered by my great aunt, carried on by my mother. She was the unofficial costumier for community theater productions and regional historical pageants for nearly fifty years, as was my great aunt before her.

Mother remembered where she bought and how much she paid for the living room rug. She pointed out an old love seat I'd never liked. She said it came on the boat with an immigrant ancestor from England five generations ago. Suddenly the soft pear wood held a brighter and deeper sheen.

There was no end to such stories—several lifetimes relived, renewed, repaired, unrepairable.

By the formal closing on October 31, my mother said she was ready to go. She kept some bread and cheese and soup in the refrigerator until the end.

The eight-week moving process was exhausting yet exhilarating as the family revisited so much we had forgotten except in our bones, rediscovered secret pleasures we still did not care to share.

When our time comes to move from our house, how will we handle it? Will we be able to throw out the stacks of neighborhood newspapers, mementos from school pageants, meeting minutes of non-profit organizations? Will we pass on the children's report cards and college notebooks now in boxes in the basement? Can we open to our children the letters we exchanged that college summer?

I am not ready for any of this yet.

But I have learned that I shouldn't wait too long for the final house cleaning. It is better to do it with the children, but only when they are old enough to understand that there is much they did not know. That your life was both the bedrock you worked so hard to create for them to stand on, and also the passionate rockiness of their own experience—molten and shifting, regrets mixed with no regrets, passions loosed and choices made and the living and mute consequences of those choices. And it all goes back very, very far, and forward farther.

Two Letters

(December 1995)

Big hulking college graduates sit around our kitchen table this Thanksgiving vacation. They have been hanging out here during vacations for the last seven years, raiding the refrigerator, playing mini-basketball at the plastic hoop over the back door and talking to each other and—increasingly—to us.

They are the same four boys we have watched grow up all through high school as school mates, team mates, close friends of our son and now of our family.

One, a recent graduate of Johns Hopkins University, works delivering pizza and bussing tables at a restaurant. Another, a graduate of Marquette University, cuts flowers at a flower shop. The two others are still in college, both taking a fifth year, hanging on to youth as long as possible.

All four are obsessed with the question: What will they do next? The Johns Hopkins graduate is wondering if medical school is really where he belongs, even though he can dissect a rat's brain as easily as a pizza maker slices pepperoni. He loves architecture, yet feels he may not have the courage to create the designs he feels inside him.

The flower cutter has no idea what he will do. Possibly pursue a teaching certificate. Or go into business, where his father says there are good opportunities. What's the next step? How to take it?

The two still in college know they have successfully avoided these questions only temporarily.

I looked on, confident that their lives will work out, and I told them so. A letter I had recently unearthed in my mother's house when she moved out after forty years reminded me that I once felt exactly the same way.

I wrote the letter to my parents the summer prior to my last undergraduate year. The anxiety I expressed is intense, maddening, circular. What would I become? How would I get there? Yes, there was a woman in my life, but what did that mean? How could I marry while facing a life that loomed before me only as a black hole of uncertainty and unbelief?

"Do you realize," I wrote to my parents, "that I only have one more year of college? At the end I should have a degree. But will I believe in anything? If not, what do I do?"

Referring to the protagonist in Henry James novella, *The Beast in the Jungle,* I wrote: "I cannot, I will not be a Jonathan Marcher, a man who waited all his life for the grand experience to happen to him. His 'beast in the jungle' never came, and I sometimes fear that mine will never come. I have to make it come, but how?"

I was twenty years old. Eighteen months later I was married, had a child on the way and was deep into graduate studies. Paralyzing anxieties over my destiny had disappeared into urgent baby cries, whopping examinations and sleep deprivation.

Thirty years later, with that child now a father and our second child married and with child, the future has taken care of itself in a way that my youthful anguish could never have imagined.

Shakespeare wrote: "Some are born great, some achieve greatness, and some have greatness thrust upon them." Most of us don't brush greatness at all, but looking back, not forward, we can honestly say we have made a life.

A second letter illustrates that tale. It was handed to my son-in-law as he worked his emergency room shift in Northern Michigan just prior to Thanksgiving. It accompanied a 79-year-old man dead from a self-inflicted gunshot wound.

According to the brother who brought him to the hospital, the man had worked in the woods of Michigan all his life. He never married. When he felt his body unable to do the work he expected of it, he wrote a farewell note to his family, lay down in bed and fired a bullet into his brain.

The terse note ordered that no extraordinary medical measures be taken, that there be no funeral, no mass, and that the family should scatter his ashes in the woods behind his garage. Business done, he added this postscript: "I had a long and happy life. Mainly because of the kindness and consideration of my relations, friends and acquaintances."

"A long and happy life" sounds idyllic, but of course it can't be the whole story. No doubt he too was wracked by doubt at twenty-five. What was he missing by not marrying? What loves had he lost? What great books had he failed to write or read? What wars did he suffer in or suffer from by being left at home?

And yet, looking back, life felt "long and happy" to him. All major questions were settled due to the ministrations of "relations" and "friends and acquaintances," another name for community.

Such retrospective wisdom won't help the college boys, as it wouldn't have helped me in my pre-adult anguish. That's life. Yet I expect the college boys will be able to add such a postscript to their last will and testament, even as I begin to realize that I might be able to do so now. Only when an old letter turns up thirty years later will they be reminded, as I have been, how young and scared they were.

Crystal Trees
and Other Reflections

(January 1996)

A great gully washer poured from the evening sky. A solid spring rain, ready to soak the lawns, jump-start the tulip bulbs, clean the spring streets. There's only one problem. This is the middle of January. In Minnesota.

Neighborhood intersections flooded as water coursed down frozen streets. Cars slipped and slid. Boulevard branches drooped and dripped. Power lines dropped.

Small tree branches covered the sidewalk like broken birds' feet. An elm branch the diameter of a human torso crashed onto our neighbor's sidewalk, barely missing a power line and who knows how many evening dog walkers and prowling teenagers.

The rain first arrived inside our house as a single splash on the kitchen counter. Then another. Then three more. The kitchen light fixture was dripping.

While my wife got out sponges and buckets, I ran upstairs. The soaked bedroom floor over the kitchen confirmed that I was on the right trail.

Outside the porch door over the outdoor deck, rainwater gushed off a "V" in the roof between two dormers. It overwhelmed a special gutter I had fashioned last fall to contain just such heavy rains. I had not imagined the gutter would be filled today with ice opaque as toothpaste. I was staring at the Minnesota homeowner's familiar winter nightmare—the dreaded ice dam.

Because the gutter was frozen solid, the unseasonable rain

washed down the side of the house, flooding the deck and penetrating the rooms below.

I will not regale you with our dark night of the buckets. Suffice to say that those we emptied from the porch every half-hour or so substantially reduced, if did not eliminate, the flow onto the kitchen counter.

I further stanched the leaks by shoveling the snow, now heavy as wet cement, off the roof deck and chipping a trail in the ice for the water to flow to a still functioning gutter.

Due to the all-night diligence, I am happy to report that the kitchen ceiling did not collapse (as had the dining room ceiling a year earlier due to a still mysterious plumbing leak). Nor did the electrical system burst into flames (although we have yet to turn on the affected light to test the watery circuit).

But the effects of this wild evening were hardly over.

During the night a cold front raced through the region, dropping temperatures back through the sub-zero floor. The rain congealed, then transformed into blowing snow. Finally it stopped. In the pre-dawn blackness, the neighborhood lay frozen, bleak, forbidding, charged with negative energy.

At first light, I wobbled bleary-eyed into the kitchen to brew morning coffee. As the sun reached up over the apartment buildings to the east, I dutifully pulled open the kitchen shades. I was blinded by radiance. Sunbeams scattered through ice-covered backyard branches like lasers through crystal. Each stem and branch and madly clinging winter leaf was covered. The sun and storm turned the neighborhood trees into magic candelabra.

Since the storm, the wind chill factor has terrified parents and given Californians and Floridians further reason to gloat. Worse, neighborhood streets are better suited for skaters than for automobiles.

But the crystal trees continue to bloom and to redeem. January rain repays its pain with radiant trees, champagne dawns, electric sunsets and mercury vapor nights of the spirits.

Painful rain and radiant ice reflect as well the neighborhood's year of joys and sorrows. Several neighborhood children celebrated joyful marriages while others were tragically lost to accident, disease or despair. Several hard-working neighborhood volunteers received well-deserved public recognition for their selfless work while another—a mother and unbelievably effective community volunteer—died inexplicably of an aneurysm.

Inexpressible grief and ineffable joy. Neither was expected nor deserved, but given nonetheless. Winter rain and crystal trees surround us still.

Cardinals and Crows

(April 1996)

In early April, spring finally showed signs of becoming possible if not yet irresistible. A lone seagull floated over the barren oaks and boulevard elms looking fruitlessly for open water. A robin called out its early and unhappy arrival over our frozen lawns.

Some sidewalks on the shaded north side of neighborhood blocks remained ice-covered and treacherous, the result of January's freakish frozen rain coupled with a miserable March sleet storm.

Before the neighborhood turns its attention to the much deserved resurrection that spring surely will bring, let's recall one last time the frozen whirlwind we have just endured and honor its remarkable survivors: Our neighbors and ourselves.

The cold was blistering and constant from the first of November, reaching record lows right through this first week of April. Two neighbors on my street were caught with their stucco down, so to speak, and their houses spent the entire winter surrounded by scaffolding and plastic by probably now bankrupt stucco contractors. The contractors had planned to finish their respective stucco jobs last fall but never saw enough November days above 45 degrees F. to mix the concrete. Who knows when we shall see such balmy temperatures again so masons can free these neighbors from their prisons.

Throughout that impenetrable stretch of cold and snow, two long-time neighborhood residents buoyed my spirits. They were up and about first thing every morning, singing and playing.

I refer to *corvus brachyrhynchos*, the American Crow, and *cardinalis cardinalis*, the Northern Cardinal.

In spite of my hurry to escape the violent cold and wind as I walked the dog, I could not resist pausing to watch or listen for them. As the winter grew longer, deeper and colder, I grew more and more appreciative of the grace and persistence of their presence.

Their species have been year-round residents of the neighborhood far longer than *homo sapiens*. We should sing their praises before too many of their migratory cousins, fresh and fat from months flitting about southern resorts, drown them out with the hopeful chatter of their return.

The cardinal is not really a beautiful bird, in spite of the male's distinctive bright red body, black mask and broad, seed-cracking beak. Perhaps it's the too upright stance and the oversized crest, too much like an uptown punk. But ah, the song!

Almost every morning, a stirring, liquid beauty flows over my painful, brittle footsteps and dry, cracked skin. It isn't the phrasing – usually one or two upswept notes followed by four or five short descenders – but the purity of the sound itself. Listening is like hearing Kiri Te Kanawa, the New Zealand opera singer whose pure tones make one's spirit soar and weep in seconds even as she too sings in an unknown language.

If the descending trills of the cardinal remind me of the passionate arias of divas, the raucous calls of crows remind me of sniggering victorious pirates. Like cardinals, crows astound in the very fact of their persistent presence in the middle of our intractable winter air.

I know what cardinals eat. A pair visits our feeder regularly to pick out the sunflower seeds my daughter provides. More diligent bird feeders in the neighborhood take care of many others.

But how do crows survive in winter? Other seasons, they dine handsomely on road kill common along streets and highways—squirrels, raccoons, dogs, cats, the occasional rat. They are skilled scavengers, coyotes of the air. But in bitter winter when even squirrels don't dare leave their houses? Yet survive they do, and prosper. We humans must leave scraps enough to feed them handsomely even in a landscape so bitterly frozen.

Four crows live around my block. They call to each other in rasping bursts many mornings and comically bounce to the tips of the oak branches over my neighbor's house.

Humorous when roosting, crows fly with vigorous abandon at air temperatures in which most car engines only groan. In strong winter winds, when human neighbors lean toward radios for warmth as well as wind chill advisories, these clever, obnoxious scavengers become truly graceful, riding sudden updrafts on steady wings, playing joyously in the worst adversity. How do they do that, in air so thin and hard to breathe?

One particularly bitter morning I groaned round the block just past dawn. It was so cold the dog tried to levitate all four feet off the frozen sidewalk simultaneously, sniffing only quickly at the morning news. Suddenly a crow alighted on a rough hackberry branch right in front of us. No light whatsoever escaped from his black feathers, black beak, black feet. He was a crow-shaped negative space, a black hole in the surrounding white. As he flew off again in a mocking bustle of wing flaps, I followed his open, crow-shaped window into a parallel winter universe of powerful laughter and persistence.

If cardinals can sing and crows can fly when the wind-chill falls so low one can barely draw a breath, can our northern winter be that bad?

Of course it can. It's miserable. But it's also graceful and inspiring. The cardinals and crows teach us that.

That lesson is worth remembering in April. For even as the future resurrection of spring blesses and rewards our long endurance, winter will return soon enough, burying our streets and houses and spirits too if we do not recognize the abundant evidence of persistence and grace.

The Writer, the Reader, the Orthodontist and the Flashlight

(October 1996)

Last month's celebration of the one hundredth anniversary of the birth of F. Scott Fitzgerald, born in St. Paul on September 24, 1896, included a public reading of his collected works. I was assigned to read the short story "Absolution" with playwright John Fenn. We were to begin at 5 p.m. on Wednesday during the birthday week at Landmark Center in downtown St. Paul. Having never read the story before, how could I have anticipated that our daughter's smile would be on the line?

Early this September our youngest daughter developed serious problems adjusting to her first year in high school. Her emotional strength collapsed. She would not go through the doors.

Wild with concern, my wife and I naturally pressed on her the urgent necessity of traditional schooling with all its educational and social benefits. After all, every fourteen-year-old goes to school, doesn't she?

Then I read "Absolution."

The story is about a Catholic boy of eleven who believes he has committed a mortal sin by lying to the priest during confession. He tries to avoid a subsequent communion but is forced to attend by his brutal father. The boy is terrified. "There was no reason why God should not stop his heart" for what he believed was "blasphemous sacrilege." "He knew that it was a dark poison he carried in his heart."

Instead, the sad old priest with "cold, watery eyes" reaches deep within himself in response to this anxious, troubled child. Instead of raining down upon him damnation from the superstructure of Christendom, the priest uncovers the remains of his own passionate soul.

When the boy finally, painfully reveals his "sin," the priest pauses for a long time, then responds: "When a lot of people get together in the best places things go glimmering."

"Things go glimmering?" The boy could not believe what he was hearing. I could not believe what I was reading.

The priest tries to make the boy understand how little the details matter that are oppressing him. He paints him instead a marvelous word picture of a party where everyone is properly dressed and there are bowls of flowers. He follows with an example of an amusement park observed from a distance, "like a fair, only much more glittering." "It won't remind you of anything, you see. It will just hang out there in the night like a colored balloon, like a big yellow lantern on a pole."

And from that moment in the story—the moment the priest describes the radiant possibilities of daily life and thus delivers true absolution onto the head of the young boy—the reader too feels a weight lift from his heart.

In some cases, for some people, the silent pressures of outside structures grow so fiery hot inside that life flows out of the body like molten lead. Then, like the boy, one needs absolution: Relaxation of that weight which is the source of pressure—religious rules, family rules, school rules, social rules. Let the child stand aside for a moment and just breathe in life's radiant glimmer.

Fitzgerald's priest absolved our daughter particularly from the exhausting pressures and long-forgotten justifications of the powerful formal educational system my wife and

I had assumed to be right and necessary for her, that drove us forward and fulfilled us in so many ways.

I finished reading the story early the morning of the public reading, eager for my daughter to learn the lesson of "Absolution." Mrs. Coyote planned to bring her early to Landmark Center that evening to attend the reading.

Unfortunately, my plan failed to take into account the orthodontist. When she arrived in St. Paul, Mrs. Coyote reminded me that our daughter had a 6:00 p.m. appointment in Minneapolis, a half-hour drive away. It had been arranged months before and was impossible to change. I quietly hoped there would be time to finish the reading before they had to leave for the appointment.

Unfortunately, the reading started late as a young engineer fiddled with the microphones until ten after five while the audience assembled. "Let's go," I told John. We began the story.

John read the part of the child, I of the priest. The story conflict developed quickly and rose to the violent crescendo when the boy's father beats him for trying to avoid communion. At that point the story feels like it will turn very bad. The boy will be forced to attend communion, the priest's response will confirm the boy's fears, the boy will leave his cubicle with despairing, suicidal or murderous marks on his soul, imprinted forever. That's certainly how I believed the story would go at that point.

With disaster hanging in the air, I saw in the audience my daughter turn to her mother and tap her wristwatch. Mrs. Coyote smiled at me and shrugged. They quietly left their chairs to keep the date with the orthodontist.

Sometimes absolution takes time. The following weekend my daughter, her best friend and I took a long-planned weekend canoe trip into the Boundary Waters Canoe Area, cold and wet but with fall colors radiant, the quiet soul stirring.

The first night in the tent, with the aid of a flashlight, I began reading "Absolution" aloud to the girls.

Her best friend was snoring by the second page. My daughter stayed awake in spite of our vigorous paddle through sleet that afternoon. She listened all the way to the final image of northern young men and northern young women, full of the radiance of life, glimmering in wheat fields.

As I turned out the light, my radiant, sleepy daughter rolled over in her sleeping bag. "I don't get it," she said. I smiled as I fell asleep, believing I finally did.

PART SIX

THE END OF A GOOD SUMMER

1997–99

I Lost It in the Garage

(February 1997)

One snowy winter day an old neighborhood friend called me to complain that she had received a ticket while parked on the street near her apartment. Apparently, she had violated some arcane snow removal regulation. Of course, she said, *you* don't have such a problem; *you* have a garage!

Let me tell you about that garage, I answered. I just got a ticket too, and my garage caused it.

Here's the story.

I drove home one Saturday in early February and, because my wife's car was parked in the driveway, I parked on the street, a common, reasonable and legal practice. What appeared neither common nor reasonable was finding a ticket on my windshield when I returned to the car an hour later.

I figured it must be due to some snow plowing regulation I had missed, but since I saw no special warning signs on the street I was miffed.

A glance at the ticket compounded my pain. "Failure to display front license plate. Fine: $36 dollars."

I should have known.

The license plate was missing because the front bumper to which it was attached was also missing.

No, I had not smashed into one of those glacier-like snowdrifts that regularly constrict our neighborhood streets into cow trails. I did that last year and learned my lesson after paying more than $600 to replace the entire plastic bumper cover of my 1991 station wagon. This winter I've driven with the gingerly grace of a ballet dancer.

No, this accident was caused by the garage, plus a ladder and a son. I'll start with the son.

He arrived 24 years ago, our third child, a happy, bubbly boy. Was it a mistake to have so many children? I didn't think so then, nor even after his recent graduation from college and subsequent return to live in Minneapolis, the city of his beloved Twins, Vikings, Timberwolves, family and, not incidentally, storage space for his stuff in our garage.

We were receptive last summer when he put his snow tires in the small attic over the garage. Late this January when he finally decided to install them after several snowstorms nearly cost him his life, we were pleased when he retrieved them from the attic and this time returned the aluminum extension ladder to its proper place.

The ladder has a story too.

After a decade or more of borrowing one from my next-door neighbor Paul, I finally felt obligated to purchase my own. That decision significantly simplified my access to the gutters, storm windows and attic storage, although I missed the neighborly conversations my borrowing excursions engendered.

The new ladder created a problem of its own: How to store it in an old garage barely wide enough for two cars? I had to be careful to lean the ladder into the wall or it tilted dangerously near the car.

Back to the ticket. The Sunday following my son's snow tire excursion, I pulled my car out of the garage for a hurried trip to pick up gumbo for my first ever party for the Super

Bowl, in which my beloved Green Bay Packers were contestants. As I hurried off I saw my wife waving her arms frantically. I thought she was warming up in the Arctic cold. I waved back.

I discovered in the restaurant parking lot what made her so excited. My front bumper hung nearly off the car, swinging freely like a badly torn fingernail. What the…? I pulled it off the rest of the way and placed it in the back of the car.

Limping back home, hot gumbo in hand, I gazed warily into the dark recesses of the garage. The aluminum ladder lay on the garage floor against the garage door track. So that's it. When I had hurriedly pulled out of the garage, the front bumper hooked the ladder, sliding it back until it struck the garage door track and stopped, peeling back the bumper like a knife blade under a fingernail.

I have since paid several visits to my friend Paul Hagen at Hagen's body shop on Lyndale Avenue. He has a salutary history of cobbling together inexpensive repairs out of broken plastic body parts. No luck this time. He can't reattach the bumper cover because all the attachment brackets were broken off. A month later Paul is still searching for a used bumper cover for me - "You can't believe what they want for a new one!" he says. I can believe it, I tell him. Plus $36 for the parking ticket, I say to myself.

So my friend, should I be grateful for that garage? That ladder even? And for that son, who at least returned the ladder to the right place, albeit leaning the wrong way, a sign that the years of training in manners and etiquette are finally paying off in general if not in the particulars?

Certainly I should. And yet when I hold in my hand that $36 ticket for "failure to display a front license plate" and contemplate the looming bill to display a front bumper, my gratitude escapes me. Instead, I find myself clawing at the leaden sky.

So, you called to complain about a parking ticket?

She began to laugh. She laughed louder. Then I laughed. We both laughed and laughed until the sound of our tears splashing on our telephone receivers drowned out our midwinter madness.

The Problem With No Name

(June 1997)

The winter of 1996-97 began early and hung on late. Spring seemed frozen, the earth's turning stuck at the Ides of March all the way to June.

For some parents in the neighborhood the frost came even earlier and lasted longer. Like prematurely aged celestial stars, our adolescent girls collapsed in upon themselves. A toxic combination of their scrambled feelings, insights and frailties plus today's virulent social and cultural climate made their step from childhood to adulthood perilous enough to cause them to stumble and fall.

Some adolescent girls saw themselves in their mirrors as hopelessly overweight although others saw them as thin. Others bought tubes of make-up products to control acne imperceptible to others but mountains in their minds. Many froze parents out of their conversational lives while chatting effortlessly on-line over the Internet with anonymous peers or perverts.

Their sense of self collapsed into mute, paralyzing fear resulting in anorexia, bulimia or refusal to go to school, or exploded into angry multi-colored braids, bolts through the tongue and flirtation with the dangerous social extremes of easy sex and drugs.

Their relationships with parents became a battle of wills which the children instinctively knew they could win. The children had the trump card: They did not think they cared if they died.

An army of therapists advised parents to put their distant, disaffected children in the hospital, or ply them with the latest miracle drugs, or both. They advised the children to take ownership of their failures and control of their fears.

The children just sat—mute, sad or angry.

Such was the case this year with our youngest daughter. At 15, she spent much of this school year in bed, unable to cope with school and her changing world. Formerly a conscientious, admirable student, she completely lost her traction. She was like a car without snow tires stuck in a winter ditch, rocking back and forth, wheels spinning hard but unable to gain any forward motion.

Neither she nor several therapists could tell us anything useful about her anxieties. We asked her again and again, what's going on inside you? She would open her mouth but could find no words.

We were hardly alone wandering in this mystery of modern adolescence. Whenever I was among other parents and mentioned our daughter's collapse, at least one in the group would jump in, "Mine too, mine too!" And not just daughters. Many strapping adolescent sons are inappropriately angry, violent, unapproachable or self-destructive.

Our daughter's particular behavior, it turns out, even has a name: "school refusal." Doctors at the University of

Minnesota are formally studying this behavior for the first time under a grant from the National Institute of Mental Health.

After this school year of mystery, my wife and I still don't know when this plague of adolescent anxiety and self-destructiveness will end. But we have gained some sense of its causes.

As psychologist Mary Pipher makes clear in her helpful book, *Reviving Ophelia: Saving the Selves of Adolescent Girls*, the world in which our children are growing up is not the same as the one in which we parents became adults.

In this column a decade ago I described the despair I felt while walking hand in hand with this same daughter outside the first local video store. Pornography or its close cousin was in sight behind the counter and posing on bus billboards outside the door. The streets pulsed with the boom box hustle of passing cars proclaiming come-hither tales of overt aggression, violence and lust. This was a cultural landscape substantially debilitated from ten to fifteen years before when we raised our first three children.

In the intervening years that beat has only grown louder. Intense magazine and newspaper cover stories openly discuss rape, incest and sexual violence, long overdue and healthy for the adult community but leaving children the impression that everyone from strangers to priests to parents are potential predators, undermining the trust basic to healthy growth. Epidemic public discussions of sexually transmitted diseases add a frightening poisoned thorn to the spring bloom of love. Pervasive marketing of products to children, too often through images of sexualized adolescents, offers them only false economic, social and sexual empowerment.

Most adolescents find ways to resist such influences.

Others, smart girls particularly, internalize the massive weight of these inappropriate and contradictory messages, and collapse. Mary Pipher describes their condition as a "problem with no name."

The collapse of adolescent Ophelias involves many other factors to be sure, certainly including the child's unique bio-chemistry and her family and community circumstances. But it almost certainly represents a defect in the culture as well. Our wide-open culture invites our young to a darkly prurient feast their bodies are not yet able to digest. Confronted with that dilemma, many children either grow up too fast or refuse to grow up at all.

Then, just as mysteriously, they revive.

By Christmas, our daughter had dropped out of two schools, ignored a kindly tutor who came to the house, and confounded a psychologist and a psychiatrist. Then, as we despaired for solutions, one day she connected her feelings to words.

"I don't know what's happening to me, and I don't like it," she said to her mother one evening. "But I know I'll get through it. The only thing I need is the one thing no one will give me."

"What's that?" she asked.

"Time," she answered. "I need time."

Time. Hearing that word was like hearing air released from a pressurized tire. Time. We can give her time.

For the first time in four months, our household relaxed, able to imagine again a future in which our daughter would regain her traction and launch herself back onto life's winding road. It would only take time.

As we relaxed the pressure on her to go to school, she regained color in her cheeks. Sometime during the spring—

after two more false starts at less pressurized "alternative" schools and our refusal to hospitalize her in spite of an official suggestion that we do so—we gained confidence that this frightening phase was passing for our daughter as it does for most.

Summer has finally arrived, green and warm. Our daughter has a job scooping ice cream at Sebastian Joe's ice cream parlor a few blocks from our house. She pops up promptly at 6:00 a.m. to go to work. She's joined a rowing club and works out daily on the Mississippi River. She's studying French at Alliance Français.

Yes, she still sleeps too much sometimes. And we have no clear idea what the next school year will bring.

But the solution to reviving Ophelia, "the problem with no name," now at least has a name. We call it "Time."

On a hot day, stop in and order a cone from this recent survivor of the adolescent wars. Her smile and sense of humor are again dazzling. We're proud of her. And, frankly, proud of her parents. We've had a long, hard winter. But the summer is wet and sweet.

The End of a Good Summer

(August 1997)

The State Fair has closed. Apples grow heavy in the orchards. A tingle of red already tips some boulevard maples.

Rilke wrote of this time of life.

Already the ripening barberries are red,
and in their bed the aged asters hardly breathe.
Whoever now is not rich inside, at the end of summer,
will wait and wait, and never be himself.

We first came to this neighborhood more than a quarter century ago as our family's spring began. Since then we've raised four children within a single block of our current house at the corner of Girard and Lincoln avenues. All are flourishing now, surprisingly tall and strong and flavorful.

The community gracefully offered us a chance to grow. We gained strength through work with the neighborhood schools, political organizations, youth athletics, arts organizations, adult teams, many voluntary associations of men and women, and this volunteer newspaper. These were the gifts of a place powerful enough to attract and hold a citizenry committed not only to individual economic vitality but also to the shared task of growing community.

Because of living here, we are rich.

But as our children finally vacate our house after 30 years of our parenting, and two grandchildren now leave their singsong voices on the voice mail, a change of seasons is in the air.

The Hindus say there are four stages of life. The first, student, and the second, householder/career, are now falling behind. The third stage begins, according to Hindu tradition, around the time of the birth of the first grandchild. No word exists in English for this phase (nor for the fourth, the renunciation that comes with complete understanding and acceptance), but when one enters it the rhythms of the body and the mind turn inward toward questions about life itself.

One day when our second son, now 25, was a toddler,

I walked him in his stroller around Lake of the Isles. Finally my feet could not contain their joy at such a summer and I broke into a run, pushing him laughing with glee ahead of me. I've been running here ever since.

Walk again, the legs say now. Take the plump hand of a fresh grandchild and go at his pace. The body now says, bend down to visit the glistening spider webs at the edge of the trail. The eyes now say, look up at the stars, overhead all along, and plunge into their mysteries. The hands now say, dig up old stories of grandfathers never known, and of places only imagined. The ears now say, listen for the music coming from deep underwater, the music of failure (as poet Bill Holm wonderfully puts it) as well as of success.

Above Lake Superior is a smaller lake called Nipigon. From it a white water river flows south. On a boulder in the center of that river stands my grandfather, who died when I was four. I see him clearly in an old photograph taken there. But who is he, really?

This past August on Lake Superior's Michigan shore, our eldest daughter, her husband and their baby son gathered a bowl of ripe wild blueberries no bigger than hatpin heads for my 53rd birthday pie. They could hardly force themselves to leave that beautiful spot near the mouth of a north-flowing river said to have two hearts, the blue burst so brilliantly in their mouths.

It's close to time for me to pay those places a visit myself. To find out, finally, from which river, which heart, life really flows.

For the Urban Coyote, the asters of fall are beginning to bloom.

Will You Be at Home This Halloween?

(October 1997)

What are you going to be for Halloween, a curmudgeon or a sorcerer? That is the question that bedeviled me this particular October, and for the first time I didn't readily know the answer.

All my remembered life I'd been a sorcerer on Halloween. As a child I stalked the neighborhood streets of DePere, Wisconsin, a masked creature holding my sisters' hands or rambling with my tricky friends. A generation later I walked the streets of our urban neighborhood holding the hands of each of our four children dressed as unraveling mummies, idyllic brides, powerful witches and bloody vampires. My wife and I reveled in the opportunity to conjure up Halloween anticipation and excitement for them the way so many did for us as children.

Halloween is the one occasion we Westerners are allowed to cross identities with the shadow world. On neighborhood streets, children transform themselves into characters from ancient and fantastic stories. They flirt with terror while wandering dark streets with packs of like-minded undead. What a rush! I thought I'd be a Halloween sorcerer forever.

But this year, for the first time in thirty years of parenthood, my wife and I have no children living at home. Our youngest daughter finally found that a boarding school is the right place for her. We found the right one. She walked in and never looked back.

Now no young ones swirl around the house during the last week of October pondering the question: What should

I be? No one ransacks attic closets in search of our secret stash of miniskirts, hippie love beads, high heels and wedding veils.

This year, instead of requests for costumes we received an invitation to a surprise birthday party for a new friend who just moved to the neighborhood. The invitation required us to costume ourselves on Halloween Eve! Now I was the one pondering the question: What character from the other world might I become this Halloween?

A curmudgeon. That's the only answer that came to me.

A Halloween curmudgeon is one who turns the porch light off, not on, as the sun sets on October 31. The one who hides in the back of the house in the dark, refusing to answer the door chimes, tending his own secret stew-pot of misery. The one too busy with personal machinations and misfortunes to care about community rituals, even one so delightful for children.

In the small town of my childhood, one such curmudgeon's house stood out. It never had the front porch light on for Halloween. We kids suspected the dour couple was secretly at home in spite of the darkened door, for a suspicious light emanated from the back of the house. But the doorbell, which we rang fruitlessly every year, remained unanswered. Tricked out and greedy, and with all the wisdom of adolescence, we egged the place.

Forty years later, I realize that I might have misunderstood that dark and silent door. Perhaps the couple were taking care of sick relatives. Perhaps they were sick themselves. Maybe they truly couldn't afford the candy tribute demanded by the costumed, aggressive hordes. Maybe they sneaked down the block to attend an adult party, enjoying a well-deserved respite from the parenthood wars? Maybe they weren't, in other words, curmudgeons.

With that insight came another. Maybe we *could* attend our friend's Halloween party without committing a misdemeanor against neighborliness. After all, aren't there plenty of younger parents on the block to light up the porches and fill the Halloween sacks for marauding, insistent children? Didn't our block party this year positively swirl with younger parents and their aggressive little offspring? Wasn't a bouncing baby born right across the street just as our youngest child left home for school this fall? Who could possibly miss one single house light at the northeast corner of Girard and Lincoln Avenues this Halloween?

I could, that's who.

Over the years I have built an experience at our threshold that thrills the goblin hordes, their parents and, yes, me, even if it terrifies Mrs. Coyote. Here's what trick-or-treaters now expect at our front door.

A hideous electronic laugh emerges from under the welcome mat (a cheesy battery-powered five-and dime device, but it makes kids smile every year). At the sound of the doorbell, a tall, hairy creature peers out at startled trick-or-treaters through the front door glass. It wears a coyote skin hat, a shaggy white beard and (now) reading glasses. Terrifying.

The front door creaks open (an ongoing problem with the hinges). Inside, a real coyote (stuffed) howls in the center of the hall surrounded by blazing candles (the part that makes my wife crazy). A headless one-armed, one-legged creature (a dressed up old seamstress dummy) guards the scene. The hall resonates with ringing Tibetan brass bowls, bone-rattling Australian didgeridoos and wild wolf howls (tapes) while the mystical scents of jasmine and sage cloud the air (cheap incense).

A cackling voice (due to an especially bad cold this year) summons trick or treaters to accept "the coyote challenge."

Come in, children. Touch the wild coyote. Good for you, there's one KitKat. Dare to shake the empty sleeve of the headless household guardian and there's a mini-Snickers for you. A peanut butter cup is yours if you have the courage to extract it from the coyote's howling jaws! (This last challenge, which I thought would be terrifying, has proven exceedingly popular. The brasher visitors, usually boys, enjoy pulling out the stuffed coyote's rubber tongue as well.) A bonus if you'll pet the tarantula walking on my shoulder (which jumps the moment they reach for it, assuming the duct tape still covers the hole worn in the rubber air activator).

Neighborhood parents tell me their children look forward every year to the Urban Coyote's Halloween test of courage. So do the parents themselves, even when a few of the youngest goblins immediately pivot and run crying for parents' knees (was it the runny nose under the Coyote headdress?). They all come back the next year. And the next.

No, I can't leave my front door unlit this Halloween. I have not yet fully repaid the anticipation and excitement others gave me with their porches brimming with light. Their doors opened, and I confronted safe, intoxicating fear. Trick or treat, I'm a sorcerer still.

The Visitor From the North

(November 1997)

"Augusto! Augusto!" the shoeshine boys called out as we walked across the Plaza de Armas in Iquitos, Peru. They ran up, chattering in Spanish with wide smiles, flip-flops slapping their heels, wooden shoeshine boxes clattering over their shoulders, shiny black hair freshly combed.

Augusto's mother greeted the boys, José and Oscár, as friends, hugging them both while they prodded Augusto's tummy as he sat in his stroller and laughed with delight.

Augusto's grandfather, a white-bearded visitor from the north, stood next to them, and shook hands when his daughter introduced him as Augusto's abuelo. "Buenos diás, Jose. Buenos diás, Oscár. Mucho gusto. I have heard much about you."

They walked on together, the visitor, his daughter and grandchild and the two young friends. They walked past the central fountain with the statue of an Amazon River pink dolphin, past the crumbling high-rise office building abandoned by Americans, past the air-conditioned Banco de Credito, past the famous building with an elegant tin façade mistakenly sent from France a hundred years ago to Iquitos, Peru instead of Quito, Equador, on to the Cafe Express for fresh papaya juice, coffee and fried egg and cheese sandwiches.

The cafe, marked on the outside only by a weathered Coca-Cola sign, held six small tables. A television set jabbered from the back wall next to a framed photo of the proprietor dressed in a starched high collar, a portrait of the Virgin Mary and two calendars featuring buxom naked women. The waitress, a handsome woman with bobbed dark hair, fussed familiarly over Augusto and his mother as we entered.

The visitor from the north took it all in. He drank his black coffee, ate his toast with egg and cheese, and listened to his heart.

This young mother, his daughter, lives here. Now quite comfortable speaking Spanish, she handles herself, her friends and her fat, happy baby effortlessly. Her hard working husband studies malaria in nearby rain forest villages. She radiates a profound and almost sleepy contentment.

It was not always thus. Not in Peru nor in her life.

The first month in Iquitos had been very hard, she told her father later over a lunch of fried catfish overlooking the Amazon River basin. She and the baby became sick immediately upon arrival. They could find no proper housing. She knew little Spanish. The money was strange, the motorcycle taxis loud and smelly, the days fiery hot, the nights dripping hot. And since she had encouraged her husband to take the job in such an exotic location, she endured a special sense of failure that she was not keeping up.

Her father had heard nothing of these problems before.

But now they live in a quieter apartment. José, Oscár, the waitress and many others fuss over them as valued friends. Wilma, a giggly, slow-eyed speaker of Castillian Spanish, is an eager baby-sitter. Irma, with a heart as big as a capybara (a gentle, dog-sized jungle rodent), takes Augusto into her bustling, cheerful home at any moment's notice. Babbi, an American Baptist missionary who trained as a civil engineer, cheerfully offers rides when needed in her dusty Land Rover.

The white-bearded visitor from the north took it all in, swept along by the world his child is making in the heat of the equatorial rain forest 2,300 miles from the Amazon's enormous mouth, someplace he never thought anyone he'd know would ever live.

The next day she and her husband guided him up the Amazon into the rain forest wilderness to swim with blind pink dolphins, watch slow-moving sloths and startle bright-colored birds too numerous and unfamiliar to identify. Another day he followed his son-in-law on his doctor's rounds to remote villages up an Amazon tributary as he extracted blood samples from malaria victims, to be used in the search for the malaria parasite's slow but dangerous adaptability.

He thought of the other places his daughter has lived on her journey from her parents' northern city of freshwater lakes. The day she and her younger brother walked to Kenwood elementary school and their eyes froze shut in the cold. The day she went off to Anwatin Middle School an angelic child and returned an edgy adolescent. The evening she drove off to a high school party and didn't return all night while her parents' searched for her and called the police. Her high school graduation art show that revealed the extent of her talent.

The university apartment where she fought off a brutal rape attempt. Her crowded apartment in New York City. Her Volkswagen van in which she traveled the Southwest, camping out while wrestling with her future. Her beautiful wedding day overlooking the intersection of two Great Lakes as tumultuous weather swirled around us. The remote farm in northern Michigan, her baby's first home.

And now, fully grown, her decisions, her vision, her life. After 27 years of parenthood, her father was now the tourist, his child the guide.

Minneapolis and Iquitos have something in common. Both are river ports situated about 600 feet above sea level near the headwaters of great river systems. Our waters flow together in ways unimaginable until they actually touch.

The visitor chuckled over a memory from his last night in Iquitos before returning to his home in the North. Friday night crowds swirled on the Boulevard Malécon overlooking the rising Amazon, for the summer rainy season had finally begun. A balloon seller held high her crown of colorful animals. Noisy children pushed toy automobiles up and down the short strip of paved walkway. Recorded music floated out of cafes along the street while an Andean band played guitar, drums, cane flutes and panpipes for tips. Tribal women decorated with tattoos offered handicrafts for sale, negotiating silently with the lift of an eyebrow.

A young boy, another member of the shoe shine trade, smiled as the white-bearded man walked by with his family. "Santa Claus!" he called out.

The white-bearded man smiled at the boy and to himself. Santa Claus indeed. He had sent to this place a gift from the north, his daughter and her life. And he would take back north the lightness of his giving, the relief knowing that the gift was properly delivered and received.

He listened to his heart. It pushed out from the center of his chest like a river, slow, powerful, warm, life-giving.

"Who are you really, wanderer?"

(May 1998)

Every Thursday morning three couples from the neighborhood meet at one of the local coffee shops for conversation. When we began this rendezvous nearly a year ago, we would talk about our adventures during the week, the frustrations and joys of children, jobs and community lives, topics not generally addressed in the workplace or while helping children with their homework.

But as the weeks went on, we ventured deeper into the *terra incognita* of our personal stories. Poetry helped us get there.

One morning one of the women, the shyest, whom we all knew to be in a strained relationship with her husband across the table, found a quiet moment and read to us "You Who Never Arrived" by Rainer Maria Rilke.

> *You who never arrived*
> *in my arms, Beloved, who were lost*
> *from the start,*
> *I don't even know what songs*
> *would please you.*

As she read, her inexpressible heartache broke into bloom before us.

Soon others brought poetry selections. We all began to look forward to such readings, which often echoed something deeply present in our lives but hard to say out loud.

Last week I brought the book *The Darkness Around Us Is Deep*, the selected poems of William Stafford edited by Robert Bly. I had no particular poem in mind but was under the spell of a comment I had come upon recently in a small literary magazine, *Sow's Ear*. The editor ended a moving eulogy to Stafford, who died in 1993, with this admonition: "Let us not go through a day without reading a poem by William Stafford."

Since then, I have tried to fulfill that gentle mandate. I carry the *Selected Poems* around in my briefcase and marvel whenever I read his gentle but provocative wisdom. But often I am too tired at night or too hurried in the morning to take the time.

Our weekly coffee group takes the time. Which, come to think of it, is why it exists, and why we all seem to look forward to these encounters.

I opened my Stafford book and found this poem.

A STORY THAT COULD BE TRUE

If you were exchanged in the cradle and
your real mother died
without ever telling the story
then no one knows your name,
and somewhere in the world
your father is lost and needs you
but you are far away.

He can never find
how true you are, how ready.
When the great wind comes
and the robberies of the rain
you stand on the corner shivering.
The people who go by —
you wonder at their calm.

They miss the whisper that runs
any day in your mind,
"Who are you, really, wanderer" —
and the answer you have to give
no matter how dark and cold
the world around you is:
"Maybe I'm a king."

Of course, of course, we said to each other, that's the answer we all should have inside us! Then why, we wondered, is that response often so hard to give or to believe in? Why is it that so many children and adults have no answer to that nagging question inside, "Who are you really, wanderer?"

William Stafford seems to have understood very early in his life that he had the power of a king inside him. I've often wondered how. His Quakerism may be a key, that training in true humility. Part Indian, Stafford embodied ecological and spiritual humility as well. His family's poverty taught him to look for resources within himself, not outside in the world. Whatever the causes, Stafford seems to have understood for much of his life that he carried true power within. He had the courage to conscientiously object to World War II, hardly a popular path at the time. Throughout his life he easily shared himself and his work with others without seeking anything obvious in return, just as a true king would if confident in his power.

With a busy life as teacher, husband and father of four children, Stafford found time every day to write a poem. In some quiet corner of the house late at night or early in the morning, he followed the thread of consciousness from whatever simple detail caught his awakened eye to wherever it would lead. Robert Bly quotes William Blake to illuminate Stafford's process:

> *I give you the end of a golden string,*
> *Only wind it into a ball,*
> *It will lead you in at Heaven's gate*
> *Built in Jerusalem's wall.*

Each week, we wanderers around that coffee shop table find ourselves holding the golden ball of a poem in our hands. Doing so seems to unlock us. Good poetry helps us past private silence to arrive, each in his or her own time, at the only answer to the question, "Who are you really, wanderer?" that makes any sense at all, no matter "how dark and cold / the world around you is:/ 'Maybe I'm a king.'"

This Newspaper You Hold in Your Hands

(June 1998)

The Hill and Lake Press is put together by volunteers. Neighbors gather in the Kenwood Park Center several evenings each month to cut, paste and chat. On rare occasions a joke or juicy story distracts a volunteer's attention from a page and a strip of type is pasted slightly on top of another, or a small strip of an article falls to the floor to disappear among the other scraps.

So when several lines were missing from my column last month, leaving a sequence of lines seamless to the eye but senseless to the reader, I laughed in instant recognition of how the error came to be.

Laying out the Hill and Lake Press is like assembling an Amish quilt. Amish women "gossip" throughout the many days spent sewing brightly patterned cloth one side to the other. That gossip is in reality an exchange of valuable community information. The resulting quilt therefore represents not only something to warm a bed but also an embodiment of the community that made it.

The Hill and Lake Press newspaper that appears on doorsteps and in local retail outlets ten times a year embodies a similar double information exchange. The conversations during the editing and paste-up processes are as much a part of the community as the newspaper you hold in your hands.

Like any true gift, this newspaper comes from the heart. And any heart gift has a flaw, for the heart is wise and does not understand perfection. This is why Navajo weavers make sure a flaw appears in their tightly woven, patterned rugs. The flaw reminds the weaver and the recipient that the work of human hands can never be perfect. From that understanding the sweet milk of community can flow.

Neighbors sew our community quilt from a large and colorful variety of small initiatives. They coach children on soccer and t-ball fields, attend PTA meetings, serve spaghetti at the school banquet. They work with the young and old in churches and synagogues and community centers. They pass out petitions urging neighbors to pay for better street lighting, or serve on committees to fight crime and improve the local landscape. They convene endless neighborhood meetings in a vain attempt to slow commuters' automobiles racing through our streets.

No one is forced, or even expected, to do any of this. When the organizer of the softball league calls and says there can be no team for your daughter unless you coach, the love of your child breaks your bonds of shyness and restraint and sense of an overwhelming workload, and you hear your lips answering, "Yes, I will." When a proposal for an inappropriate high-rise threatens the neighborhood's character, you find yourself at a neighbor's kitchen table forming a neighborhood organization to fight it. And when the neighborhood needs a way to communicate its own information, concerns, celebrations and grief, you find yourself working with others to paste a small monthly newspaper together.

And what is the payment for all this? Well, there's high school graduation, for one, when the children you have helped play and work and learn stand together swaying like fat reeds along a lakeshore and you find tears of joy coursing down your cheeks. Or there's the moment when the team that once barely recognized a soccer ball makes a goal and the children hug each other with joy, and you feel your chest swell. Or when this newspaper appears on the doorstep and you have taken part in making it, it glows for you.

So when a small flaw appears in the layout of this community newspaper you hold in your hands, the product of so much love, it unexpectedly becomes a conduit to that love. And I am again reminded that so many have opened their hearts by giving us this gift from their hands.

On Going a Journey

(February 1999)

"One of the pleasantest things in the world is going a journey; but I like to go by myself."

William Hazlitt, *"On Going a Journey,"*
Table Talk (1822).

As a salesman during the Depression, my father drove from small town to small town selling coal to cheese factories. All that travel time alone should have been hard for such an ebullient, sociable man. Yet his mind was joyously occupied, he told me. He had learned important travelling lessons from William Hazlitt's essay, "On Going a Journey," which he remembered clearly from his high school English class.

He recalled often and with particular relish Hazlitt's comments on anticipating dinner. "I grant, there is one subject on which it is pleasant to talk on a journey; and that is, what one shall have for supper when we get to our inn at night.... Every mile of the road heightens the flavour of the viands we expect at the end of it." Dad laughed the many times he recalled that particular passage to me, licking his chops as he eagerly savored each element of a fantastic upcoming meal.

Before he died in 1985 at the age of 81 of a heart attack after eating lobster and dancing late with my mother and other zesty ladies, he gave me his worn copy of the essay. I never found the time to read it until now.

I expected the essay to contain many more of the sociable reflections so delicious to my father. I was surprised, therefore, by Hazlitt's opening line, " *One of the pleasantest things in the world is going a journey; but I like to go by myself.* "

It turns out that Hazlitt loved the solitude occasioned by a walk between towns. His private ruminations and reflections then could live without interpretation or translation to others. "Oh! It is great to shake off the trammels of the world and of public opinion—to lose our importunate, tormenting, everlasting personal identity in the elements of nature, and become a creature of the moment, clear of all ties...."

Until recently such a reflection would have appeared strange to me. For me, the pleasantest way to go a journey has always been "in company." Which was fortunate because I have always lived in company. First my family, then my high school and college friends, then my wife and our four children were always on the trip. We all wanted it that way. In fact, the pressure inside my chest to take my family with me on any excursion was almost unbearable. During the instances when I did travel alone, I longed to show them what new places I had found, wished they too had the experience, felt incomplete without them. Like my father before me, I would send home descriptions of what I found on the road. "Let us share our adventures together," we wrote.

I also loved and needed the community. Why would we do anything alone if we could do it with friends and neighbors, I wondered?

But now that our children have fledged and flown after 32 years of parenting, 25 of those years in the Lowry Hill neighborhood, I felt a powerful attraction to the singular pleasures of traveling "by myself."

Now underway on a three month writing trip to California, I feel exactly as Hazlitt said I would. "Then long-forgotten things, like 'sunken wrack and sunless treasures,' burst upon my eager sight, and I begin to feel, think, and be myself again."

"By myself" I can "be myself" in ways necessarily put away a generation ago for the proper fulfillment of family and community obligations. Now I have the chance to fulfill my idiosyncratic interests as well. I can stop the car by the side of the road to watch an unfamiliar bird or inspect the carcass of a roadkill without fear of waking a sleeping child. I can listen to the books and lectures on tape I choose without the battle for control of the car radio that used to cause so much family static.

And so I did. Driving three days to Arizona, I listened to taped lectures on poetry and mythology and to Tom Wolfe's fat new novel, *A Man in Full.* On the radio I chose the soothing effects of classical music, which I long to better understand. Occasionally I surfed by the familiar commentators of "All Things Considered" on National Public Radio and shuddered with annoyance, relieved I was not listening to that night's recap of the all day live coverage of the impeachment trial of President Clinton.

Instead, I stopped often by the side of the road with my binoculars. I kept a journal, writing down as I drove the random thoughts and observations that bubbled up "like sunken wrack and sunless treasures."

In Arizona, where I conducted interviews for two weeks, I had time to hike desert trails alone at sunset. I paused in the presence of fat hummingbirds needling into blossoms of unfamiliar trees and pricked up my ears as coyotes chorused nearby. In California where I am working now, I pick ripe oranges off the ground early in the morning. Wasted here, to me they make the sweetest juice.

I could only leave on such a journey "by myself" because my family is grown and healthy, the neighborhood well tended. My wife is richly occupied with WATCH, the organization she started seven years ago in response to a murder in the neighborhood. It has grown into a nationally recognized model for helping the court system better respond to the social afflictions of sexual violence and domestic abuse. Our older children have put down roots, some deep, some still exploratory, in New Mexico, California and Malawi in southeast Africa, while our youngest daughter flourishes in her boarding school.

In the neighborhood, a new generation of families of all

kinds is digging in, fixing up the remaining old houses and voluntarily participating in the activities that nourish their environment and each other. They are busily discovering what my family discovered over our 25 years living there, that strong neighborhoods create an invisible web of supportive relationships that help raise the next generation while raising our expectations of each other and of ourselves.

Driving south near the Iowa border, I pulled off the freeway. I looked around the crowded rest stop and saw no one I recognized, nor even familiar clothing or body types. I realized then that I was finally beyond the powerful magnetic field of the family, the neighborhood, the Twin Cities metropolitan area: My roots, my home. Only then did my travelling spirit break free as Hazlitt said it would. After half a lifetime building familiarity and relationships to set the future free, I now was free myself. Free to travel where unnamed birds flutter, where unknown trees grow and unfamiliar animals sing in the night. It's time for me to howl their stories.

THE END

About the Author

Jim Lenfestey has worked as a college literature instructor, director of an alternative school, sales manager for an environmental company, consulting editor for an urban American Indian newspaper, marketing communications consultant to high tech companies, playwright, and editorial writer for the StarTribune where he won several Page One awards. At Metropolitan State University he taught courses in American Indian Literature and the Literature of Comedy. He and his wife Susan raised their four children in the Lowry Hill neighborhood of Minneapolis, where he helped found the Hill and Lake Press and an association of neighborhood and community newspapers. For fifteen years he authored a monthly column, *The Urban Coyote,* which won numerous "Best Ongoing Column" awards from the association. His articles, poetry and short stories have been published around the country. His play, "Coyote Discovers America" (with Jon Cranney) premiered the 25th anniversary season of the Minnesota Children's Theater. He and Susan currently live in Minneapolis and Mackinac Island, Michigan. This is his first book.